TALISMANIC MAGIC

TALISMANIC MAGIC

Robin Skelton

Samuel Weiser, Inc.
York Beach, Maine

First published in 1985 by
Samuel Weiser, Inc.
Box 612
York Beach, Maine 03910

ISBN 0-87728-553-5
Library of Congress Catalog Card Number: 84-55291

Typeset in 11 point Bembo by
Positive Type, Millerton, NY
Printed in the United States by
Interstate Book Manufacturing Group, Olathe, KS

Contents

List of Illustrations vii
Introduction xi
Chapter 1
What is a Talisman? 1

Chapter 2
Identity Talismans 11

Chapter 3
Organic and Found Talismans 21

Chapter 4
Traditional Talismans 37

Chapter 5
Talismanic Stones 57

Chapter 6
Inscriptive Talismans 75

Chapter 7
Astrological Talismans 101

Chapter 8
Kabbalistic Talismans 111

Chapter 9
The Consecration of Talismans 133

Chapter 10
The Nature and Use of Talismanic Power 143

List of Illustrations

Figure 4.1 Hand of Fatima, 38
Figure 4.2 The Egyptian talisman of the *udjat*, 40
Figure 4.3 The Scarab, 40
Figure 4.4 The *Ab,* 42
Figure 4.5 The Egyptian *Ankh,* 44
Figure 4.6 The swastika, gammadion or fylfot, 44
Figure 4.7 The Sauvastika, 45
Figure 4.8 Some variations on the Sauvastika, 46
Figure 4.9 Greek or Equilateral Cross, 47
Figure 4.10 The Latin Cross, 48
Figure 4.11 Other variations of the Latin Cross, 48
Figure 4.12 The Mandala, 50
Figure 4.13 The Yin and Yang, 50
Figure 4.14 The Pentagram, 51
Figure 4.15 The Hexagram, 51
Figure 4.16 Hexagrams of the Elements, 52
Figure 6.1 Alphabet of Honorius the Theban, 84
Figure 6.2 Alphabet of the Magi, 85
Figure 6.3 The Three Angelic Alphabets, 86-87
Figure 6.4 Ancient Numbers Symbols, 88
Figure 8.1 Tree of the Sephiroth, 112
Figure 8.2 Table of Saturn, 124
Figure 8.3 Kamea of Saturn, 124
Figure 8.4 Kamea of Jupiter, 125
Figure 8.5 Kamea of Mars, 126
Figure 8.6 Kamea of the Sun, 127
Figure 8.7 Kamea of Venus, 128
Figure 8.8 Kamea of Mercury, 129
Figure 8.9 Kamea of the Moon, 130

To Jean Kozocari

Introduction

Although there are many books about the history and practice of magic, there are very few about talismans alone, and there is no comprehensive survey of the subject. This book is an attempt to remedy this situation, to reveal the part talismanic magic has played and continues to play in human life, and to help people interested in exploring the subject to create talismans for themselves.

Magic itself has been defined by Aleister Crowley as "The science and art of causing change to occur in conformity with the will." In other words, magic is a way of making things happen without using physical or mechanical means, but by employing psychic energy. This energy may be directed by a person (as when a priest, shaman, or healer cures or alleviates a disease by means of a spell or the laying on of hands), or it may operate through an object which possesses and transmits the energy (as when the relics of a saint cause miracles to occur).

Belief in the "magical" has been supported by all religions. Holy objects and relics, including priestly vestments and ceremonial robes belonging to men of authority, have always been regarded as having magical power and as being talismans. It was not until the industrial revolution and the growth of so-called rationalism in Western Europe that magic began to be regarded as stupid superstition by large numbers of people, though the power of magic was never completely denied. In the twentieth century, however, man has come to realize that there are energies and forces at work that we know very little about, that the symbolic systems of the so-called "occult sciences" do give us a picture of forces that actually affect human existence, and that these forces may well be as closely connected to the movements of the stars and consequent changes in the natural rhythms of life as astrology supposes. It has also been shown that every thing possesses an energy field which can be photographed by Kirlian photography, and that the energy fields of living things are continually altering. These fields have been, in the case of plants, translated into electrical impulses which can either be seen on a screen or heard as sounds. If a plant is threatened by a person simply *thinking* of harming it, its energy field alters. It may even stop "transmitting." We now know therefore that all things transmit "vibrations" and that where living things are concerned, these vibrations can communicate emotional states at the very least. The nature of transmitted vibrations is not yet fully understood, but they are as real as radio waves, which were discovered and labelled not so long ago. Vibrations appear to communicate at unconscious or subconscious levels. They do not appeal to the conscious self. When we react against a house or even a person and speak of "bad vibes," we cannot explain the nature of the "vibes," however powerful the effect may be. We get the message, though, and those of us who are especially sensitive and intuitive get the message very clearly indeed.

Talismans send out vibrations. Sometimes these are made doubly effective and communicate with us at a deep level because we recognize consciously that the talisman is related to a religious belief, myth, or legend that has fascinated mankind for hundreds of years. We are moved, for example, by the image of the cross, not only because it may refer to Christianity, but because the cross has been an important symbol ever since records of man existed. Somewhere deep inside us we keep a personal record of our evolution as a race, and what moved us in the beginnings moves us now and is part of our psychological make up. Thus these ancient symbols form a language that speaks to what Paul Huson has called our "deep mind," and as it is the deep mind which is the very foundation of our beings, this language can affect us profoundly.*

Modern psychology and parapsychology and the recent discoveries of the neuro-biologists and the practitioners of Kirlian photography explain in part why talismans can affect us, and perhaps why there is an increase in the popularity of talismans in

---

*For more information regarding deep mind, refer to Paul Huson's *Mastering Witchcraft*, G. P. Putnam's Sons, New York, 1970.

our time. Nowadays the wearing of talismans, amulets and charms is not only socially acceptable, but fashionable. The ankh, the Egyptian symbol of everlasting life, is worn as a pendant as frequently as the cross. Many travelers and taxi drivers carry medallions of St. Christopher with them wherever they go. And the signs of the zodiac are present everywhere in the form of pendants, rings, brooches and stencilled T-shirts.

Most people would agree that medals of St. Christopher and crosses and ankhs are generally regarded as having protective qualities. Few, however, would say that a coat of arms or a pin indicating membership of a particular club had any magical significance, and yet the reason for wearing or displaying these is to warn off some people and encourage others. They therefore do have a talisman-like effect. They make things happen "in conformity with the will." Moreover, because there is obviously a difference between using talismanic symbols as a form of social communication and using them for magical purposes, it is not always easy to make the distinction. A man may wear a military uniform because this establishes his social function, but the wearing of the uniform may give him an irrational sense of personal power. It has been said that "the uniform makes the man," and there are many instances where people have been punished for "insulting the uniform" as if the uniform was possessed of personality and had virtue in itself.

Talismans have long been a part of human life, and over the centuries many different kinds of talisman have been created, some of them extremely simple and some of them very sophisticated indeed. Not everyone will want to create the most sophisticated ones, but if we are to understand the nature of talismanic power and talismanic thought, we must explore these as well as the talismans in common use. In so doing we will find ourselves establishing a series of general principles that can be used in making talismans ourselves. No one book could, of course, survey all the known talismans, for every country in the world has its own list, and in many cases these talismans are made from materials peculiar to the individual country. I have chosen, therefore, to deal mostly with those talismans found in North American and European cultures, or in the most ancient ones of the Mediterranean and Middle East from which western civilization largely developed. I have not included those talismans which are intended to play a part in ritual magic rather than simply to protect or otherwise affect the owner or wearer, but I have done my best to explain the basic notions of astrology, Kabbalism, and the doctrines of signature and correspondences which form the foundation of much ritual magic as well as of much talismanic theory.

In working on this book I have helped by a great number of people, and must particularly thank Jeffrey Gould, Sam Llewellyn, William David Thomas, John Robert Colombo, and Patrick Grant for directing my attention to matters that I might otherwise have missed. I am also, as always, deeply grateful to my wife, Sylvia, who has provided the illustrations.

Robin Skelton

Chapter 1

What is a Talisman?

If God is the creator, and lord of created things, how is it that the talismans of Apollonius have power over parts of creation?

Attributed to St. Justin Martyr
A.D. 150.

Talismans, amulets, and charms are usually regarded as being quite distinct from each other. Talismans are objects which confer power of various kinds upon those who wear them or own them. Amulets, properly speaking, are intended to protect their owners from both physical and psychic illness and from misfortune. Charms combine the functions of both talismans and amulets but consist only of written or inscribed words or symbols. Despite this, many objects regarded as powerful talismans and amulets contain or include inscriptions, and it is often difficult to say whether or not a given object is an amulet or a talisman, for some objects have both active and protective functions. For the purposes of this book I have used the general word Talisman for all these objects in order to avoid unnecessary complications and confusions.

A very long time ago, stone age man drew pictures of the bison hunt on the walls of his cave in order to ensure a successful hunt. This is an instance of sympathetic magic; by imagining a successful hunt the stone age man felt that it was certain to occur, and by imitating it graphically, he was bringing his image to life. The same kind of magic is at work in the ritual dance, in which the dancers act out the drama of the thunderclouds coming and the rain falling in order to cause rainfall, or the magic inherent in country superstition that you can cause rain by spitting on a stone, imitating the arrival of the first raindrop. The drawing of bison hunt, even though it is also an instance of sympathetic magic, is still talismanic, for it is an object with magical power.

It was not long after this first use of sympathetic magic that talismans began to appear. At first they were probably objects that represented the powers of nature which were regarded as gods, or demons, or other kinds of spiritual beings. The earliest objects were very simple, but as time went by they became increasingly elaborate. A crudely carved stone might at first be regarded as an image of a god and therefore as having the power of that god. Just as saying the name of the god was believed to bring that god into the speaker's presence, so every image of a god was thought to be imbued to some extent with the god's power. This is the kind of talisman we have in the St. Christopher medal, in ikons, and in religious medals. Johannes Lalas of Antioch reported in A.D. 550 how Apollonius, in order to rid Antioch of scorpions, made a bronze image of a scorpion, buried it, and built a pillar over it. Soon after, all the scorpions left Antioch.

These talismans need not all bear actual representations of the god, saint, or sacred personality whose power are intended to influence, or of the animals, insects, or disasters they are made to affect. Some of them make use of graphic symbols which represent the god without portraying him; an obvious example is the Christian cross, which does not have the figure of Christ upon it. Sometimes the symbol might refer to a particular incident in the life of a man of power or saint, or a part of a god only. Thus there are Egyptian talismans depicting the *Udjat*, or Eye of the Moon God, and a Syriac talisman of King Solomon spearing a devil.

Such symbols were thought to have some power in themselves, but not very much. After all, they were not images in which the god or the power lived, but reminders of those images. The sacred images themselves only could answer prayers and grant wishes if treated well with food and drink and a good house, and some of them seemed to respond especially well to feasts that involved dancing and bonfires and the sacrifice of an animal or even a human being. Images which conferred power upon the possessor and which protected him from ill without his having to actually pray or worship probably developed from the belief in the ability of the gods to bless, to give power to, an object; this power would then reside in the object itself. This kind of talisman is frequently found in societies that contain a powerful priesthood. The priest, or shaman, or witchdoctor has the authority to give power to the object by blessing it in the name of the god, or by placing it in a holy place such as the god's shrine for a certain length of time. Talismans of this kind are usually created for protective purposes, either general or specific, depending on the nature and particular interest of the god concerned.

In the middle ages a great deal of trade was done in the bones of saints, pieces of the true cross, and fragments of saints' garments under the supposition that something once connected intimately with a person of psychic power and charisma would provide its new owner with some kind of protection against the powers of darkness. The relics themselves were also believed to have the power to bring prosperity and to heal sickness, and shrines containing relics were the object of many pilgrimages.

The belief that a relic of a person of power has power is not entirely dissimilar to the belief that objects which symbolize one's guardian spirit or patron saint are talismanic. People in many societies have felt that there are spirits watching over them, and have often thought these spirits to be those of their ancestors. The person who could claim people of power and charisma as ancestors was regarded as having inherited their power and being under their protection. Parents handed down personal objects of adornment to their children, not as wealth, but as symbols of the family's strength and importance. People also began to boast of their lineage, and to symbolize it in images and drawings. The Indian totem poles of the Pacific Northwest portray the lineage of the family or person to whom the pole belongs, usually in terms of the various guardian spirits that have been, as it were, "in the family." The banners and heraldic devices of nobility show by means of symbols something of the lineage of their owner. These symbols refer to historical events, to persons of consequence, and to people's trades or professions. They are talismanic in their assertions of the family power, the strength of the guardians. Those who carry them or wear them feel protected.

These kinds of talismans—the holy image, the blessed object, the relics and the heraldic device—seem to have been the first kinds to be generally accepted. There were, however, others which had nothing to do with the worship of a god or with inherited power. These were simply "found objects" that were so strange or so interesting in shape that they made the finder think they had magical power. They had personality; they had charisma; and mankind has always regarded personal charisma as being a kind of magical power. Roots shaped like the male genitals, silver or golden coins that have been pierced or twisted, stones which have holes through them—all these have been and still are regarded as having magical powers of one kind or another. Some found talismans may be quite without interest to anyone but the finder. Those of us who pick up pebbles and shells on the beach know well that every once in a while we find a "special" stone which we regard with great pleasure and treat as a treasure, and that the reason for this cannot usually be explained to other people.

All the kinds of talisman I have so far described are connected either with a straightforward belief in natural forces and spiritual powers or with a belief that oddity and charisma are themselves magical, and we can all sympathize easily with these beliefs. It may be less easy to accept talismans which are based upon elaborate symbolic systems, such as the Kabbalah, or upon specific religions. Nevertheless, these talismans can be effective, for many of them make use of words, names and inscriptions which have universal significance. The use of words and names of power, perhaps the name or names of a god or spirit or a quotation from a holy book, was and still is extremely common. Many of these talismans are immediately intelligible. A talisman to protect one against blindness, for example, might contain the essential part of a story of Jesus healing the blind; a talisman to protect the wearer against ill fortune might include the name of a sun god, which, once recognized, could easily be accepted as significant.

When we move on from either the symbolism of a widely known religion or the simple use of easily identifiable names, to the use of talismans based upon the elaborate mystical systems of secret societies, we are brought face to face with a knotty problem: is it essential to believe in or at least sympathize with the system of belief underlying the talisman for it to work? With talismans, are we dealing only with the magical, or psychic, power of faith? Or, even if we do not believe in the system behind the talisman, does that talisman have power itself? Is it possible for an object to alter actuality by its spiritual energies?

There is no doubt at all that faith plays a great part in talismanic as in all kinds of magic. If you believe that a talisman has power, then you yourself adjust your own psyche so that it sends out the appropriate messages. If you feel you are protected, and feel it strongly, then you are granted self-confidence and courage. A great many of the ills of life are caused by our own psychic imbalance, and we can "refuse" to be healed and can "insist" on medicines being ineffective. The talisman against disease, either in general or particular terms, sends a message to the subconscious or "deep mind" of the individual and obliges it to respond by directing the body to heal itself or to counter the disorder. Thus faith in talismans is not simply superstition—it is a mode of directing psychic messages inward to the deep mind and commanding it to help and heal. Faith in the talisman is an important part of its power.

As with protective talismans, so with active ones. If you have a talisman which is credited with leading to success in love, and if you believe in the talisman, then your deep mind will transmit telepathic messages which are of the kind to make success in love possible or even probable. If you have a talisman for success in money affairs, then the wearing of it will cause your deep mind to so order your thinking and your attention that you will have the success you desire. In these instances the talisman derives its power from the wearer's belief in it.

What about talismans that are not believed in? This is a more difficult question to answer, for scepticism and downright disbelief will always fight against the success of any magical act. It is not much use wearing a talisman for prosperity if you don't believe in it. Your doubt of its efficacy is also a doubt as to the likelihood of prosperity arriving. Therefore, the deep mind may well get a negative rather than a positive message. If your doubt is particularly strong you may even find that the magic reverses itself and causes misfortune to befall you.

Not all talismans, however, require the faith of their possessor. It is possible to imbue a talisman with power, and for the talisman to function quite autonomously. If you wish to give a love charm, for instance, you must first of all imbue it with the messages you wish it to carry. You can do this simply by writing the words on the gift itself. A woman receives a bunch of red roses, which are emblematic of passion, together with a card that makes the message explicit. The explicit message, because it is consciously understood, can be consciously rejected; the message that the roses transmit direct to the deep mind of the recipient is harder to deny because it is harder to identify. It is, as it were, in code.

That objects can be transmitting stations for psychic potential seems now to be generally accepted. As we have seen, the discovery of Kirlian photography has led to our realizing that every object on this earth has an energy field surrounding it, and that, in the case of living things, this energy field is constantly changing. The patterns of flares surrounding a living leaf alters if the leaf is damaged or even if it is threatened. The pattern of ever changing points and flares of light around a human body will intensify if the person is emotionally excited or disturbed and will become jagged and distorted if the person is unwell. These energy fields are called "auras" by mediums and other workers in the fields of parapsychology, mysticism, and magic. It is believed by some that this aura is radiated outward from a second body which is composed entirely of energy and which interpenetrates our physical bodies. The aura perceived by clairvoyants changes as the mood or health of the individual changes, altering both its intensity and its coloring. It also seems capable of emitting messages, or "vibrations," as they are commonly called. When we say that we get "bad vibes" from a person we are saying that we are receiving messages we dislike, or even that we are being, in some way, attacked or threatened.

It is not yet proven that the energy field or aura is responsible for transmitting telepathic messages, but it seems likely since all other known energy fields emit "vibrations" and "radio waves." If this is the case, it is likely that the energy fields and transmissions of inanimate objects can be altered by charging the original energy field with energy messages of one's own. If this is the case, the talisman that has been "blessed," the "holy water" in the church front, the food one eats after blessing it in a Grace, do actually change as a result of the blessing.

Not all talismans are deliberately made. Some of them are found, and some objects not intended to be talismanic at all are used as talismans. This is particularly true of objects which send out messages because they have been, in the past, associated with some explosion of strong emotion, some psychic storm. The "unlucky" jewel or dagger is familiar to us from many stories; consider, for example, the story of the Hope Diamond. Its first owner was robbed by his son and died in poverty; its second owner, Louis XIV of France, permitted his mistress, Madame de Montespan to wear it, and shortly afterwards she fell out of favor; Marie Antoinette wore it, and was executed, and her friend Madame Lamballe, who also wore it, suffered a similar fate. Later owners died in poverty, committed suicide, were murdered, or suffered other misfortunes. Just as familiar as the unlucky gemstone is the haunted house. In both instances one explanation of the phenomena is that "messages" of great power have been left behind in these objects or places by the psychic forces which at one time affected them.

This brings up an important point about talismans, and especially about those bought in stores: if your talisman has been in contact with strong emotional force fields of a kind foreign to the intention of the talisman's symbolism, then the talisman is likely to be weakened in power or even inoperative. Thus, if you buy a cross from a man who is a total sceptic you may find it useless. Ironically enough, it is the most widely believed in talismans that are most affected by this situation. For every shopkeeper who sells a St. Christopher medal or an ankh believing in their efficacy, there are hundreds who have no belief at all. Moreover the manufacturer or craftsman who makes the talisman may well regard it simply as a gewgaw of no interest save as merchandise. It is for this reason that many people suggest that you should manufacture your own talismans, or should use as talismans objects which, because their ostensible function is not talismanic, have not been drenched with negative impulses. On the other hand, a talisman (that has been negated in the way I describe) can be made positive again by the purchaser if he or she concentrates upon the symbolism of it with great energy and intense belief in the power of the symbol for a sufficient period.

We have seen the way in which the transmitting station of the talisman is powered by faith and/or powerful energy fields. Does the symbolism itself, however, have power? Here we are on delicate ground and there are two views to be put forward. The first one is that those symbols which have been important to man for a very long time have been made in response to needs of the "deep mind" and therefore themselves constitute a kind of language which speaks directly and potently to all of us at an unconscious and deep level. These symbols, which Jungians would call archetypes, include the mandala, the cross and the crown; the moon and the sun are also archetypes. We do not have to believe in a particular religion to feel the power of this language. We react intuitively and at a deep level. These images, which Jung at first called "primordial images" and later "archetypes," represent the fundamental forces at work in the "deep mind" and picture our most powerful instincts and intuitions about life. Jung says that they "occur with great regularity; everywhere we find the idea of a magical power or substance, of spirits and their doings, of heroes and gods and their legends."[1] He points out that these archetypes appear in many religions and differ only a little from one religion to another. He suggests that we have inherited the powers they represent and the experiences they symbolize along with everything else that makes us members of mankind, and says that "The deposit of mankind's whole ancestral experience—so rich in emotional imagery—of father, mother, child, husband and wife, of the magical personality, of dangers to body and soul, has exalted this group of archetypes into the supreme regulating principles of religious and even of political life, in unconscious recognition of their tremendous psychic power."[2]

These images are so rich in meaning that it is hard for us to see any of them as having only one significance. The symbols of

[1]C. G. Jung, *The Structure and Dynamics of the Psyche*, 2nd edition, Princeton University Press, 1969, p. 137.

[2]C. G. Jung, *The Structure and Dynamics of the Psyche*, 2nd edition, Princeton University Press, 1969, p. 156.

Father, King, Queen, Sword, Cavern, and Mountain are so broadly significant that if we use them for talismanic purposes we must attempt to narrow down their symbolic possibilities to those that are relevant to the situation. Other symbols speak to us with only a little less power, and are almost as universally appreciated, because we associate them easily and immediately with aspects of our experience. We cannot but feel that anything golden has to do with the sun and with light; we cannot help feeling that bright green has a message of growth. We accept that black has to do with the loss of light, with darkness. And so forth. This kind of symbolism is almost universally understood, though it is obvious that green, for example, might be a more powerful color to a desert dweller than to an inhabitant of a country where lush vegetation is taken for granted.

Irrespective of their method of operation, these symbols are powerful in that they present messages exactly as do verbal statements, but unlike most verbal statements (with the exception of great poetry), they speak directly to the deep mind. I cannot emphasize too strongly that it is the deep mind which is the real source of magical messages and powers. The deep mind is actually the transmitter and the receiver with which we deal when we speak of talismanic magic.

We now have three kinds of talismanic power to consider: that energized by belief; that created by deliberate or chance subjection to a strong energy field; and that caused by the presence of an ageless and universal symbolic language. We have surveyed, briefly, the origins of talismans and talismanic thinking and have seen how talismanic thought developed naturally from a belief in the power of the imagination and the reality of the spiritual world. We can now go on to look in more detail at the various kinds of talisman and discuss ways of making them, and of making them work.

Chapter 2

Identity Talismans

> *...a Device exposeth the rare conceipts and gallant resolutions of its Author, far more perspicuously, and with more certainty, than Physiognomy can, by the proportions and lineaments of the face.*
>
> Henri Estienne[1]

Perhaps the most common talismanic objects in use today are those which identify the wearer as a certain kind of person. Many of these devices are only minimally talismanic in that they are intended to display publicly and explicitly some personal characteristic or fantasy, or denote membership in some social group. They are talismans in that they protect the owner from misunderstandings and sometimes lead to useful or entertaining personal encounters. They might be called Identity Display or I.D. talismans.

We can pass quickly over such I.D. talismans as T-shirts labeled with facetious messages, but we should recognize that those which say "Gay Liberation," "Pennsylvania U," or "Up the I.R.A." do indicate significant social attitudes and can therefore lead to social contacts of the desired kind. They are displays similar to the mating displays of some birds and animals who endeavor to attract mates by "showing off."

Crests, badges, and men's ties are I.D. talismans similar to T-shirts—albeit without the obvious written message. If we see a man wearing a regimental tie we know something of his background if he is entitled, of course, to wear it. The "old school tie" message

[1]From *The Art of Making Devices*, translated by Thomas Blount, 1646.

proved very effective in establishing relationships in the past, though nowadays many people may wear a second hand tie and are completely ignorant of its significance to someone who knows the symbolism.

Different societies have different I.D. talismans, some of which are intelligible only to members of the same group. Thus, only a Shriner is likely to understand all the various marks of rank and function that are worn in shriner parades, and only a boy scout will interpret correctly every one of the badges worn by another scout.

All I.D. talismans are related to the practice of heraldry which developed to its most sophisticated state in Western Europe. Heraldry began with the creation of seals that could be used to sign and authorize documents. Richard I of England was the first English King to use a Royal seal. This was in 1189. His second seal, of 1198, became the basis for the Royal Coat of Arms of England. These seals, which were sometimes large and weighty and sometimes in the form of rings, were I.D. talismans in that they displayed the personal identity of someone signing (and sealing) a document. Because these seals included symbols of power[2] they were truly talismanic; anyone disobeying the law or command thus sealed was opposing spiritual as well as earthly authority. Seals of this kind remain in use today, and business corporations and societies have registered seals.

The first actual coat of arms that we know of is that of Geoffrey of Anjou, whose father-in-law, Henry I of England, gave him a shield on which were painted six golden lions. From this time onward the nobility of Europe, the great landowners and feudal princes, began to make use of I.D. or heraldic shields, and when members of two noble families married, their children combined the designs of their parents' families in another shield. The science of heraldry, or "armory" as it should more properly be called, developed rapidly after this, and soon the rules for creating and devising shields, badges, and heraldic charges were regulated, and it became an offense against the law to carry a shield or bear a device

[2]See Chapter 6 for a more detailed discussion of inscriptive talismans.

to which one was not entitled. In a number of countries there are still special courts to deal with these infringements. As recently as 1949 a French family successfully sued a champagne company for using the family arms on their labels!

We are not concerned here with the legal aspects of heraldry, but with the way in which heraldic devices are I.D. talismans. In the fourteenth century, Joannes de Bado Aureao in his *Tractatus de Armis*, said that heraldry existed simply to distinguish one person from another. In the seventeenth century, Sir William Dugdale suggested that coats of arms were chiefly used to distinguish between families. One of the most important functions of these devices was to announce when a person was in residence in a particular house or castle, to whose family (or army, even) a person belonged, and by whose authority things were being done. This was important at a time when few people could read or write.

Because people could not read or write it was important also to choose symbols that carried a message to both the conscious intelligence and the emotions of the beholder. Thus in early heraldry we find an abundance of lions, dragons, unicorns, eagles, crowns, and castles. We also find arms that have been created by a kind of visual pun; these are called canting arms. The Applegarth arms contain three apples, for example, and the arms of the Shelley family three whelk shells, while the Welwood arms display a tree growing up out of a well. Other symbols were derived from the often hereditary official positions held by the bearer of the arms; the marquess of Ormonde, the hereditary chief butler of Ireland, has three cups in his shield. Many heraldic devices are based upon medieval lore. The lion was regarded as the king of the beasts and a symbol of kingship. Similarly, the oak was the king of the trees. This kind of symbolism depends very much upon one's accepting a certain hierarchy in the natural world, and upon the belief that certain animals, plants, minerals, birds and fish have particular ranks and qualities. It was believed in the Middle Ages and well into the seventeenth century that everything on the face of the earth had a singular, identifying quality which it had in abundance over all others. It thus became possible to represent a certain quality with absolute accuracy. The animal kingdom was thought to excel all other living things in instinct and sensuality; the plant kingdom exceeded the rest of creation in the ability to grow, and the stones and minerals were the leaders in durability.

There was also the theory that every department of creation exactly paralleled all other departments, so that for every animal there was a corresponding bird, fish, or stone; for every creature a corresponding attribute in man; for every attribute or portion of man a corresponding planet, angel, or other spiritual power. Moreover, mankind was regarded as being structurally exactly parallel to the whole universe—a microcosm. In this system of correspondences, like affects like. Thus a storm in the heavens will cause or accompany social disorder, a falling star will lead to the fall of a great man. If a lion is found dead or found giving birth, then some great prince will face either disaster or prosperity. An eclipse of the sun, the king of the heavens, prophesies the eclipse of a king; that of the moon foretells the fall of a queen. The earth itself also parallels mankind; the rivers and streams are the blood, the air the breath, the grass the hair or beard, and so forth.

This system of correspondences is far too elaborate and confused to explore in any detail here. It is, however, important to bring it into the picture for it not only lies behind many of the I.D. talismans of heraldry but also behind many other talismans. Obviously a lion will signify kingship or nobility, as will an eagle or an oak. It is less obvious however, until one thinks in terms of correspondences, that a new moon may symbolize a young princess, a star a nobleman, and a bolt of lightning, war.

Many of these correspondences may seem arbitrary to us, but they are based upon the view that any two things which are in any way similar can affect each other. This notion of the inner meaning of similarity was called the *Doctrine of Signatures*, each object, or person, bearing, as it were, the signature of the special power or virtue it possessed. Thus the lungwort, because its leaves are lung shaped and spotted like lungs, was regarded as a medicine for chest disease. Yellow flowers were helpful for urinary disorders. Roots shaped like genitalia were aphrodisiac. If a person has a chill he should be wrapped in a red blanket, for red is the color of fire. If he is feverish his fever may be lessened by wrapping him in white, for white is the color of snow. Young girls of marriageable age should wear light green or white, for green is the color of spring and of the awakening of fertility, and white is the color of the earth before the spring has begun, and therefore symbolizes purity. Men who have a store of wisdom, of secret knowledge, should wear black for it is the color of night and of obscurity (academic gowns were all, until very recently, black). Red, being the color of blood and also of Mars, the planet of war, is the appropriate color for soldiers' uniforms.

As a result of all these medieval explorations we have a system of symbolism which can be used as a kind of pictorial language both in armory and in the making of I.D. and other talismans. Unfortunately there is no one authoritative and comprehensive account of the system, and there are many disagreements among researchers from the earliest times to the present day. However, to show simply how the system works, or fails to work, Table 2.1 on page 16 and Table 2.2 on page 18 provide lists of a few of the correspondences between the natural world and human attributes that were accepted in the past. Some of them derived from myths; some are based upon natural observation—the mole becomes an emblem of humility because of its refusal to emerge into the light of day. Talismanic correspondences are different in every culture. In the East, correspondences differ because of different flora and fauna as well as different religious and mythological systems.

By no means would everyone agree with these Tables of Correspondences, and, as we shall see when we look at other talismans, many of these creatures and plants have been given other and sometimes contrary significances by different people. Even in the most flourishing days of heraldry, symbols of this kind were fully understood only by those who had made a special study of them, and therefore some heraldic devices had an esoteric significance as well as, or even instead of, a generally understood meaning. This aspect of I.D. talismans is, of course, still with us today as I have already pointed out in discussing regimental ties and the insignia of the Masonic orders. We do indeed have to realize that I.D. talismans can be either in plain language or in code.

The magical type of I.D. talisman is esoteric and intellligible only to a chosen few. Many are associated with membership in

Table 2.1. Creature Symbolism

Creature	Trait	Creature	Trait
Ant	Industry	Lion	Sovereignty
Bee	Order	Magpie	Acquisitiveness
Dog	Fidelity	Mole	Humility
Eagle	Sovereignty	Owl	Wisdom
Eel	Cunning	Oyster	Lechery
Frog	Fertility	Pig	Gluttony
Grasshopper	Frivolity	Robin	Loyalty
Fox	Cunning	Scorpion	Treachery
Goat	Lechery	Snake	Deceitfulness
Hawk	Pride and Valour	Sparrow	Lechery
House Marten	Deceit	Spider	Cunning
Jackdaw	Eloquence	Sturgeon	Sovereignty
Lark	Cunning	Tortoise	Patience

secret societies. We can separate this kind of I.D. talisman from the remainder by calling them Cypher talismans. They are, after all, in code.

For the most part anyone who wishes to wear an I.D. talisman will have little difficulty in finding symbols that are generally accepted and understood. The Cypher talisman is a little more difficult. You must ask yourself "By whom do I wish to be recognized?" and "What symbolic language shall I use?" More important still is the question which leads you from simply devising a mark of identification into creating a talisman proper. This is "How do I see myself?" or, to put it another way, "What will help me constantly to recognize who I am?"

You may feel completely satisfied by the public symbolism of an explicit I.D. talisman, having decided that you are, above all things, the member of a group, and therefore you will wear the family tartan or crest, the school or university tie or badge, and feel protected by the sense of group participation that these give you. It may, on the other hand, strike you that you will only feel comfortable if you are recognized by a select few and you will then choose to wear a Cypher talisman. You may, indeed, feel the need of an entirely personal talisman which may or may not have meaning for other people. Some people even conceal their personal talismans beneath their clothing. By doing this, the wearer provides himself with a talisman which reinforces his sense of his own identity, and improves his confidence in himself, without running the risk of betraying himself to other people. He or she may carry it concealed in a pocket or purse rather than wear it.

How can you identify yourself to yourself in such a way that the talisman continually reinforces your sense of your own unique personality and gives you confidence? There are a number of existing symbolic languages which can be used. The most obvious of the systems is based upon Astrology. You can identify yourself to yourself by wearing a talisman which carries the sun sign of the zodiac under which you were born. You can, of course, elaborate this by adding to the dominant sign the other signs, and you can even, if you wish, create a written talisman which holds the astrological map of your horoscope. This is unusual. Most people create identity talismans that only bear one or perhaps two astrolgoical symbols. This talisman is, of course, easily understood by many people these days, for astrology is popular. You may therefore prefer to create an astrological talisman by making use not of the signs themselves but of the precious metals and gemstones associated with them. I have given details of these correspondences in Chapter 5. But as an example I will pick the sign of Cancer, whose color is green, whose metal is silver, and whose precious stone is pearl. Therefore a person born under the sign of Cancer could contrive a talisman which was made of silver and pearl with a green background. Similarly a Taurean could contrive a talisman which included copper, sapphire, and pale blue. The planets also have precious and semi-precious stones associated with them. Saturn, for example, is associated with jet, onyx, obsidian, and diamonds, and Venus is associated with emeralds and sapphires. There are also stones associated with the days of the week. It is therefore possible to make up a talisman which includes symbols of the sign of the zodiac, the sign of the ascending planet, and the day of the week on which you were born.

The amount of labor and expense involved in making a talisman of this kind may well cause you to hesitate, and, indeed,

Table 2.2. Planets and Flowers

Plants and Flowers	Trait	Plant and Flowers	Trait
Acorn	Immortality	Iris	Faith
Adonis	Wealth, Longevity	Ivy	Friendship
Almond	Happy Marriage	Jonquil	Desire
Aloe	Wisdom, Integrity	Lavender	Constancy
Amaranth	Loyalty	White Lily	Sincerity
Apple	Concord	Lily of the Valley	Humility
Aspen	Lamentation	Marigold	Jealousy
Aster	Elegance	Marjoram	Comfort
Asphodel	Regret	Medlar	Timidity
Balm	Sympathy, Love	Mimosa	Daintiness
Bay Tree	Glory	Mint	Consolation
Birch	Fertility	Mushroom	Wisdom
Sloe	Austerity	Nettle	Cruelty
Borage	Courage	Orange Blossom	Virginity
Box Tree	Stoicism	Orange Tree	Fecundity
Bramble	Envy	Pansy	Thoughtfulness
Buttercup	Ingratitude	Pear Blossom	Hope
White Carnation	Pure Love	Pomegranate	Fruitfulness
Cedar	Incorruptability	Red Rose	Desire
Chrysanthemum	Optimism, Cheerfulness	White Rose	Innocence
Clover	Fertility	Yellow Rose	Infidelity
Coltsfoot	Maternal Love	Rue	Mercy
Cyclamen	Resignation	St. John's Wort	Suspicion
Cypress	Mourning	Snapdragon	Desperation
Dahlia	Treachery	Snowdrop	Hope
Daisy	Innocence	Speedwell	Fidelity
Elderberry	Humility	Sunflower	Devotion
Primula	Inconstancy	Sycamore	Fertility
Fir	Boldness	Thistle	Defiance
Garlic	Strength	Thyme	Courage
Goldenrod	Good Fortune	Vine	Wealth and Contentment
Liverwort	Confidence	Violet	Modesty
Hollyhock	Generosity	Walnut	Trickery
		Wormwood	Bitterness
		Yew	Grief

very few people choose to be so elaborate. Nevertheless, if you wish to create an identity talisman that does precisely state to yourself, if to no one else, who you are, it is hard to do so without taking some trouble over it. Astrology is not, of course, the only system that can be used to describe a personality though it is one of the most ancient.

Unless you inscribe a full horoscope on your talisman, however, it is unlikely to be unique to yourself, for many people are born under the same signs or even at the same moment. If you wish to ensure that your talisman is unique and totally personal, perhaps the best thing to do is to use the oldest magical trick of all and inscribe it with your name or monogram. If you feel that this is too public a message, you can easily "encode" your name by using one of the magical alphabets given in Chapter 6, "Inscriptive Talismans." You might also make use of the device of Gematria, which is also explained on page 120. If you do this you will have a personal talisman which includes symbols that spell out a message only to those very few who can read them. Thus you could, if a Libran, with Venus ascending, inscribe on a disc of copper the sign of Venus together with a coded version of your name.

Of course this kind of identity talisman does not include, as do heraldic devices, any reference to your lineage, or your family tribe or race, and you may wish to elaborate it by adding a symbol which refers to this or even to your job, trade or profession. In doing so, you would, of course, be creating a totally individual talisman which would carry conviction to your deep mind. You might, however, prefer to wear it concealed rather than openly. To announce one's membership in a group is one thing, but to announce publicly the whole of oneself is another. Indeed most people choose to wear their truly personal identity talismans either wholly or partly concealed. The best way to wear them is probably as pendants hung low enough to be situated over your heart.

There is, of course, one kind of talisman which could be said actually to become a part of the wearer. This is the talismanic tattoo. Many tattoos are identification talismans, some of them obvious in significance and some not. The man who has himself tattooed with the flag of his country, or an emblem of some naval ship or regiment in which he has served, identifies himself as belonging to a particular social group with certain definite attributes. The man who embellishes himself with the name of his girlfriend, or with some expression of his affection for his mother or his birth place, is not only expressing loyalties and affections but also asserting that these are a permanent part of his identity. Tattoos are unlike all other talismans in that they are regarded as permanent. They are not; but the removal process is both painful and tedious, so when the tattoo is made the person getting it should think of it as remaining for life.

Because there is a certain amount of pain involved in being tattooed, the tattoo always implies to both the observer and the possessor that an act of courage has taken place. Consequently, a person wearing a tattoo feels protected by this emblem of hardihood. He may, indeed, actually be protected, for many feel a tattooed person might be dangerous to cross. We are not here concerned with the sociological effects of tattoos, however, but with their talismanic properties, and these are firmly believed in by members of many societies who feel that by having the group emblem upon their skin they have acquired the collective strength of the whole group. The death's head tatto common among motorcycle gangs, or other emblems such as dripping daggers labeled "death before dishonor" are more than mere insignia.

There is one further kind of identity talisman which is usually kept secret. This is that talisman to which you have a strong attachment because you feel intuitively a certain kinship with it, even though you cannot see any real reason for the feeling. It may be a stone you have found, or even a colored bead. It has no obvious symbolic significance. It has no name. And yet it spoke to you when you found it and you knew it was your own entirely personal thing. These found talismans are more difficult to explain than talismans which are deliberately made or bought with conscious awareness of their significance. We will discuss both found talismans and talismanic objects occurring in the world of nature in the next chapter.

Chapter 3

Organic and Found Talismans

Chase evil spirit away by dint
Of sickle, horsehoe, hollow flint.

Samuel Butler[1]

While many found talismans are entirely personal to the finder, some are generally regarded as having talismanic power. Obvious examples are four leaf clovers, cast horseshoes, and stones with holes through them, these last being known variously as hag stones, holy stones, witch-stones, and mare stones. These are all protective talismans that bring good fortune, and there are many such recorded in folklore. Some of these derive their power from having once been part of a creature with desirable attributes. The Eskimo who sews the head or feet of a hawk into his son's clothing is intending to give the boy the strength, keen sightedness, and hunting skill of the hawk, just as in adding a piece of fox dung or fox skin and a piece of skin from the roof of a bear's mouth he is commanding the fox's cunning and the bear's strength to assist the child. Some African tribes follow a similar practice by adorning the young male child with necklaces made of the teeth of predators. Sometimes these talismans are intended for protection against the animals of whose bodies they are made. A man might wear a leopard's claw as a protection against leopards, a shark's tooth to ward off sharks. The belief here is that by wearing these talismans one is identifying oneself as kindred of the leopard or the shark and,

[1]From *Hudibras*, Book 2, Canto 3, pp. 291-292.

therefore, as their friend and not their enemy. The Dogrib Indians take this a little further by using a talisman of antler points which, while intended magically to assist in luring deer within striking distance by suggesting to the deer that they are kindred, may also have the effect of partial disguise. For the most part, however, the talismans of this kind are usually sympathetic; the Indian girl who is given a necklace of beaver teeth is given it to make her as industrious as a beaver, and not to persuade beavers to regard her as one of the family. Keeping fragments of the animals one has killed on one's person or in one's house is certainly talismanic in origin. The foxhunter who has foxes' masks mounted on his walls may be displaying evidence of his prowess; he is also, however, bringing the fox's virtues into his home, and ensuring that he retains his hunter's cunning. Similarly, the big game hunter keeps the heads of lions, buffaloes, bears and elk, or makes footstools of elephants' feet and umbrella stands of ivory tusks. He is, whether he realizes it or not, indulging himself in sympathetic magic and in talismanic thinking.

Many organic and found talismans can be explained in terms of the doctrines of correspondences and signatures in Table 2.1 on page 16. A complete listing of all known talismans and their correspondences would involve just as many conflicting views. I present a list of some of the most widely known organic and found talismans grouped together under their functions. They are further grouped under the main headings of Talismans to Increase Confidence and Sense of Well-being, Medical Talismans, Talismans that Affect Other People, and Talismans Used in Magical Rituals.

Talismans to Increase Confidence and Sense of Well-being

These talismans are particularly effective if the wearer has faith in them; belief goes a long way in ensuring their success. This list includes talismans to protect people from evil spirits, ghosts, the evil eye and to prevent disaster—these are also calculated to increase self-confidence and lessen vulnerability.

To gain personal power: Wear an eagle's feather. The eagle is generally regarded as the ruler of the sky and those that wear an eagle's feather will be able to fly high and far and be successful in their ambitions.

To gain courage and confidence: Wear a sprig of stinging nettle or thyme or provide yourself with a picture of snakes or dragons.

To protect yourself from theft: Wear a sprig of mugwort or place it over the door of your house.

To get your wish: Wear a cap woven from hazel leaves and twigs.

To gain eloquence: Wear a Jackdaw's feather. Jackdaw's feathers were often worn in the caps of itinerant beggars and entertainers in the Middle Ages. The Jackdaw is, of course, a garrulous bird.

To ensure safe journeys: Carry the feather of a lark. The lark is associated with St. Christopher, the patron saint of traveling, and also with the Sun god whom he continually praises, rising high above the earth to sing when the sky is clear.

To ensure good fortune: Have the image of a black cat tattooed on your body, carry a sprig of holly that has been used in Christmas decorations, or carry a lotus blossom, a sprig of mayweed, a leaf of shamrock or a four-leaf clover (five-leaf clovers are unlucky). You may also wear a cap made of hazel leaves and twigs; this is particularly effective for sailors and others connected with ships. Good fortune can be ensured for the family by decorating the house with laurel and bay, or with five-petalled lilac of any color. You should not however, decorate the house with lilac that has a different number of petals, and white lilac, when not five-petalled, is considered definitely unlucky. If you keep a pace egg (an egg colored for Easter) it will bring good fortune throughout the year. You may also hang a horseshoe, points upward, over your threshold.

To ensure success as a bullfighter: Carry a clove of garlic into the bull ring; it will prevent the bull from harming you. This is a Bolivian belief.

To gain a lover: Carry a mandrake root or a root of briony in your pocket. This will bring you a new sexual partner. If a girl wishes to get a husband, she should pin a wishbone over her door on New Years Day, and the first unmarried man to cross the threshold will be the man she will marry.

To help you overcome obstacles: Carry a sprig of moonwort, springwort, or chicory that has been gathered at midnight on St. James' Day (July 25th).

To gain physical strength: Provide yourself with a picture of dragons, or snakes, or eagles, and either hang it in your room or carry it on your person. A ring engraved with these symbols is particularly efficacious. Portraits of tigers, or tiger skins, have the same effect. Additional strength in the arms can be gained by tattooing hinges on the inside of the elbows. This is specially popular with sailors who also tattoo the injunction "Hold Fast" on the fingers of the hands, one letter on each finger, the thumbs being spared.

To ensure success in gambling: Wear a tiger's tooth.

To keep ghosts away: Scatter fernseed around the house or place hyacinths in the rooms. Sprigs of hawthorn may also be effective, though some think it unlucky to bring hawthorn into the house. You may also plant lilies in your garden.

To keep away evil spirits: Decorate your house with peach branches and blossoms, or hang branches of elder or mistletoe over the doors and windows. Branches of arbutus, a tree once considered sacred to the Roman Goddess Cardea, if hung in a child's room will give protection from evil.

To detect the presence of evil: Keep a toadstone at your side. The toadstone is a dark grey or light brown stone that sweats in the presence of evil. You can identify it by placing it in front of a toad, for if it is a true toadstone the toad will immediately leap towards it.

To protect a newly born child: Give the child salt, matchboxes, eggs, and coins of silver.

To protect horses: Tie a hag-stone to the key of the stable door or a sickle in the stable. A horse whose rider carries a whip with a stock made of rowan will also be protected from danger. If you fasten hazel wands to a horse's harness it will protect it from witchcraft.

To protect yourself against witchcraft and the evil eye: Carry a twig of a rowan tree with berries on it, or a sprig of holly picked at Christmas, or sprigs of garlic, mugwort, or rue. Rowan twigs, when tied together with red thread, keep witches away, and cross beams made of rowan protect a house from witchcraft. To protect the house for a whole year, you should pick some St. John's Wort on St. John's Day (which is also Midsummer Day) and hang it over the doors and windows. Garlands of birch, bracken stems, or juniper are also effective. When outside the house, a divot of turf carried under your hat will protect you from all forms of ill wishing, and kingfisher feathers sewn in your clothing will give you general protection from harm. Cauls are effective talismans against witchcraft also, and any house that has ivy growing upon it is protected against misfortune, unless, of course, the ivy dies, for that presages disaster.

To banish witches from the house: Hide a root of the male shield fern in the room; this will make any witch feel ill and obliged to leave.

To prevent harm to a child: Hang a peach stone around its neck, or place leaves of hawthorn in its cradle.

To prevent drowning: Tattoo a pig or a rooster on your left instep, or carry a caul.

To prevent snake bite: Carry serpentine in your pocket; the reason for this may lie simply in the name of the stone.

To protect yourself against danger while sleeping: Have the picture of an open eye tattooed on each nipple.

To protect yourself from lightning: Carry acorns in your pockets or place some in your window. The oak is supposedly the tree most frequently struck by lightning, and therefore has an affinity with it and can protect against it. Sprigs of stinging nettle, similarly used, will also protect you, for the sting of the nettle is as sharp and sudden as a lightning stroke.

Medical Talismans

The following medical talismans seem likely to work only when the individual concerned has so strong a faith that he can control his body's sensitivity to bacteria and viruses and increase his tolerance of pain.

To cure asthma: Carry a carrot in the pocket.

To prevent the ague: Carry teazles in your pocket, or sprigs of poplar or aspen.

To prevent backache: Wear mugwort in the area of pain.

To ensure an easy childbirth: The mother-to-be should wear hyacinth, and, when in labor, bind an eagle stone (Lapis Acquilaris, light brown aetites) round her thigh in a cloth bag.

To prevent a head cold: Hang a nutmeg round your neck.

To prevent colic: Carry a hare's foot. Samuel Pepys used this talisman.

To prevent or ease cramp: Hold a piece of cork in your hand, wear a talisman made of coffin nails or a hinge or handle from a coffin, or carry in your pocket the small bone from a leg of mutton or lamb, or take brimstone sewn into a linen bag into bed with you and hold it in your hand.

To cure croup: Carry a carrot in the pocket.

To prevent convulsions: Wear a ring made of a silver coin collected at the Communion Service or Mass, or one made of three nails or screws taken from a coffin buried in a cemetary. If the person to be protected is a girl, the talisman should be made from five silver sixpences, or other silver coins, given by five unmarried men, who are not to be told the reason for the gifts.

To cure gallstones: Carry a carrot in your pocket.

To prevent or cure gout: Carry a mole's foot.

To prevent or cure hemorrhoids: Take a ride on a donkey.

To cure or prevent headaches: Wear the skin of a dead adder in your hat. Cast-off skin will not suffice.

To cure insomnia and ensure good dreams: Wear a wreath of violets or hang one at the head of the bed.

To cure lunacy: Place buttercup flowers in a linen bag and hang it around the patient's neck. The buttercup, being the color of a newly risen full moon, will counter the moon's influence and ease the patient's mind.

To increase a mother's milk: Let her wear a sprig of saxifrage between the breasts.

To increase cow's milk: Fasten a bough of hawthorn to the door of the cowshed on May Day.

To improve the memory: Wear a wreath of rosemary.

To prevent muscular pain: Wear a sprig of spruce next to the skin.

To ensure pregnancy: Place a root of mandrake or briony beneath the bed before you make love. Pots of basil in the house will bring children to those who wish for them. Japanese women carry fragments of stone to ensure fertility. If the lady is a virgin, she should wear, on her wedding day, a bracelet of shells or a garter of straw—wheat for a boy, oats for a girl. If she is not a virgin this will not work.

To ensure a safe pregnancy: A bag containing an Eagle Stone should be worn around the neck.

To prevent rheumatism: Carry a nutmeg, potato, horse chestnut or walnut in your pocket, or wear around your neck a bag containing elder pith. Alder twigs in the vest pocket are also effective, and on retiring you should place a pillow stuffed with hops under the bed. Rheumatism may also be warded off by carrying the right foot of a hare in your left hand pocket, or carrying a carrot or a mole's foot.

To cure swellings and boils and skin eruptions: Hang a plantain root around the neck.

To cure teething pains: Give the baby a necklace made of elder or of alligators teeth.

To cure toothache: Carry a double hazel nut in your pocket, or hang a nutmeg around your neck, or take a ride on a donkey. You can also place a mole's foot and a tooth from a dead man's skull in a bag and hang it in the fireplace.

To cure whooping cough: Place a spider in an empty walnut shell and hang it round the patient's neck, or have the sufferer take a ride on a donkey, or if feasible, a bear. You can also make the patient handle some small snails (or hodmedods) and then hang these in the chimney. The snail and spider talismans are, obviously, only partly talismanic in that the disease is presumed to die as the creatures die. This remedy is therefore sympathetic magic.

To prevent or cure sickness in general: Keep a pot of basil in the house or carry a pebble that has been boiled in a pot with potatoes. A string of onions hung in a house will also keep away disease; this is at least based upon fact as the powerful odor of the onion does destroy some bacteria. If you wish to protect a child from sickness you should hang a bag of hair from the cross on a donkey's back around his or her neck. If you wish to protect the child for a whole year you should hang a sprig of St. John's Wort round his or her neck on St. John's Day. On St. John's Day you should also, to protect all members of the household for a year, hang wreaths of yarrow in the house. You can get the same results by keeping, for a year, some hot cross buns or a loaf baked on Good Friday or a sacramental wafer that was blessed on Easter Sunday. Another general and long lasting talisman against all sickness is made by first collecting thirteen coins from as many friends and then exchanging them for a more valuable and larger coin (preferably silver) which has been given to the church; this large coin should then be hammered into a suitable shape by the blacksmith and worn around the neck.

Some medicinal talismans utilize plants which either have or were once thought to have healing properties when used in potions or poultices. Spruce, for example, has been used to make a Spruce

Tea which cures scurvy, and the water in which plantain leaves have been boiled has been used to bathe inflamed eyes. If a plant has a medical virtue of any kind, it was believed that this virtue would also operate talismanically. Many doctors in rural areas in both Europe and Africa have told how their patients have chosen to make necklaces of pills and capsules rather than to take them internally; some have even used bottles of medicine as pendants. These talismans have sometimes proved to be effective; presumably they work in the same way as placebos.

Talismans that Affect Other People

The following talismans are a brief list of those talismans which, when given to others of your social circle, will affect their emotions and attitudes.

To make a person lecherous: Give him or her a sparrow's feather.

To increase a person's loyalty to you: Give him or her a rose of any color.

To make a person lose the way: Pin a sprig of fern to his or her clothing.

To gain a man's love: The woman should give him a sprig of basil.

To gain a woman's love: The man should give her a sprig of heliotrope.

To bring a person good fortune: Make him or her a gift of a large apple on Hallowmass.

Talismans Used in Rituals

One further group of talismans remains to be considered. These are not perhaps talismans proper in that their use is usually accompanied by magical rituals. Nevertheless, to round out the picture, here are three of these.

To discover hidden treasure: Carry a root of mandrake or briony.

To gain the second sight: Carry a Caul. Cauls were highly regarded as talismans in the early nineteenth century, and would sometimes change hands for as much as twenty pounds sterling in northern England.

To become invisible: Use root of Mandrake or briony or chicory; the exact instructions how to use them are unfortunately lost.

Found Talismans

There is one kind of organic found talisman which cannot be put on a list because each talisman is unique and its properties depend upon its unique character. This is a found object which appears to have no particular symbolic character but which so fascinates the finder that it is believed to have power. A great many stone talismans are of this kind. Precious and semi-precious stones, of course, are almost all regarded as talismans, but they are not true found talismans. (See Chapter 5 for further discussion of gemstones.) The found stone's power appears to be given it by the wearer who is often also the finder. It may therefore be thought that it is entirely personal and useless to other people. This is not necessarily the case. The great investigator of gypsy lore, C.G. Leland, tells a story of having found an attractive black pebble that was greatly coveted by the gypsies he met. They also coveted three patterned sea shells, one of which had marking on it that could be read as NAV which, in Romany, means "the name." The gypsies told him that they had a talisman for curing seriously ill children which consisted of three Maria Theresa silver dollars hung around the neck under the child's clothes. The Maria Theresa dollar was accepted as having talismanic power not only by the European gypsies, according to Leland, but also by members of many African tribes.

Found talismans are usually regarded as lucky charms or bringers of good fortune, rather than as having specific properties, unless the shape of the found object is extremely suggestive. Stones which resemble perfect spheres or eggs are very much in demand, so much so that many people are now busy manufacturing stone eggs as curios for fashionable stores. Whether made of common or of semi-precious stones, they are regarded as having talismanic properties. It is said that the actress, Carole Lombard, used to carry a smooth round pebble to bring her good fortune. Oddly shaped roots and vegetables turned up by the spade or found in the garden are also regarded as lucky. Potatoes that are shaped like animals or human beings are treasured. There is almost no area of phenomena in which the odd and apparently unique is not regarded as having talismanic power. This is particularly the case with coins. The Turnbull family of Northumberland (England) possessed, until the third decade of the nineteenth century, a famous Black Penny, which had a raised rim and was a little smaller than the current penny, and this was used to protect and heal cattle. It was dipped into a stream that ran from north to south and then water from the stream was given to the cattle. Another coin that was used to heal and protect cattle in this manner was the silver piece belonging to the Lockerby family in Dumfriesshire (Scotland). The "Lockerby Water" was even sold as a medicine in the 1840s. Yet another strange coin was the Lee Penny. This was actually a groat of Edward I with a dark red stone set in its reverse side, and it was used to cure hemorrhage and rabies as well as diseases in cattle. It was once even used to attempt to stop the spread of plague in Newcastle (England). In 1638 Sir James Lockhart of Lee was tried for witchcraft by the Synod of Glasgow because of his using this talisman. He was, however, judged not guilty because "the custome is onlie to cast the stene in sume water, and give the deseasit cattil thereof to drink, and qt the sam is dene wtout vsing onie words, such as charmers and sorcerers vse in thair unlawfull practicsess..."

Those who acquire oddities such as these may not think to use them talismanically, or even think of them as talismans any more than do the big game hunters who collect trophies, but they do regard them with awe, with pleasure, and with affection and consider them to be lucky. The luck, the good fortune, has of course been part of them from the moment of discovery. On picking up the pebble, the coin, the strange potato, the finder tells himself "this is a bit of luck," "this is good fortune" and, by some quirk of the mind the object itself is regarded as actually being, or possessing, the good fortune it has brought. It has been imprinted by the delight and awe felt at its finding. I must emphasize here that only objects so odd as to appear unique are usually felt to be talismanic in this way. While finding a hundred dollar bill would be indeed good fortune, the bill itself would be regarded as a talisman by only a very few people. Found coins are probably only talismanic if out of date, foreign, rare, twisted or bent.

While those of us addicted to beachcombing or who walk invariably with our eyes to the ground may still acquire talismans without having to pay for them, most of us now find our talismans in shops. Indeed, apart from antique shops and junk shops in which traditional manufactured talismans can always be discovered, there are curio shops and "tourist traps" which are happy to provide anyone with "good luck charms." Many of these are somewhat bogus. The four-leaf clover, or shamrock, which is a potent protector and whose four leaves symbolize fame, wealth, success in love, and health, when purchased in the form of a brooch is as likely to have been made in Japan as in Ireland. The miniature talismanic totems of the northwest Pacific Coast sold in tourist shops are often of the same origin. Nevertheless, the power lies at least partly in the belief of the buyer, and if the buyer sees this object with the awe and delight of the true talisman finder it may well be for him the fortunate talisman he needs.

I have spoken several times of the power of belief, but have so far not attempted to define the exact nature of the belief. At first blush one might think it is a simple thing; one simply believes that the found object has talismanic power, and therefore by believing this one provides the power oneself. This is not the whole of the story, however. One does not believe in a talisman in the way in which one believes that one and one make two, or that hitting a drum with a drumstick will make a noise, or even that the day following Sunday is Monday. These beliefs are born of experience and habit, and they are beliefs in an unchanging and inevitable pattern of cause and effect. Belief that a found object is a talisman, however, derives from a sudden feeling of a sympathetic connection with it. The feeling is often expressed that the object was simply "waiting for me" as if it were a long lost friend, or as if an appointment had been made. The object was waiting for us, it belongs to us, it is there by appointment with us, as the sword in the stone awaited the boy that was to become King Arthur of the Round Table.

This feeling is often very strong indeed, and is sometimes also connected with a particular time in one's life. It is not unusual for someone to find something which either symbolically or in practical terms exactly fits the need of the moment. This has been called, first by Horace Walpole, the spirit of Serendipity—the faculty of discovering something by happy chance. It may not however be wholly chance. Almost all collectors of objets d'art, rare books, coins, and postage stamps have experienced the power of Serendipity too often to believe it to operate at random. Many have "known" that a given bookshop actually has a rare book they need; sometimes they even have an accurate intuition of the authorship of the book. Assiduous collectors, indeed, know that at those periods when they are most inclined to build up their collection these serendipitous events occur more frequently than when they have let their interest lapse for a time. The history of all collectors in all fields is crammed with stories about these discoveries. One book collector I know was once browsing idly in a second hand bookshop when he became convinced that there was a book he particularly wanted somewhere in the shop. He looked along the shelves and could find nothing of interest. And then, as if directed by some strange command, he put out his hand and pulled out a grubby brown paper envelope, and discovered inside it one of the three scarce pamphlets he had been longing for to complete his collection. It seemed almost as if the psyche had sent out a kind of radar to enable discovery to take place.

This is, I believe, exactly what happens. When a collector makes a discovery, or when a person finds an object that he immediately knows to be a personal talisman, it is because the psyche has felt a need and responded to it. It is easy to see how the collector's find satisfies a need. It is not so easy in the instance of the talisman, for the talisman finder may not know consciously that the need exists, and it may even be that the discovery defines the need.

Found Talismans as Pendulums

The nature of the talisman, once it has been found, is not always immediately clear. The finder is only sure of the sympathetic connection; but what, exactly, is this pebble's power as a talisman? What, exactly, does this bent silver coin signify? Usually the finder simply feels that there is good fortune in it. Sometimes, however, the conviction that the talisman is not only a bringer of good fortune but a container of wisdom, leads the owner to use it as an oracle. Many owners of "lucky" coins toss them heads or tails to help them make decisions.

A similar use is made of found talismans in pendant form. To accomplish this, the truth seeker should hold the pendant by the chain, preferably by the ring clasp, so that there is no inhibition of movement in the chain. After deciding what kinds of pendular movement mean yes, no, and no answer, the individual steadies his or her arm on a table to keep it absolutely still, and asks questions. If the pendulum is a success it will soon begin to swing either left to right or forwards and back, or in a circle or ellipse clockwise or counter-clockwise. It does this apparently of its own volition, for the hand suspending it is absolutely rigid, or feels and appears to be so. Pendulums have been used in finding lost people or hidden treasure. Held above a map of the area to be explored, they will describe a circle, the center of which is the place sought.

In working with a pendulum in this fashion one must try to be absolutely free of all prejudice as to the answers that are likely or desirable, for it is possible by sheer will power, and without physical movement of any kind, to change the pendulum's direction. The pendulum, indeed, appears to operate in response to unseen and undetectable impulses from the user. These may be akin to electrical impulses, for the most effective and lively pendulums are made of materials that are good conductors of electricity or that can themselves, like amber, retain and emit an electrical charge. It seems likely that the answers are, in fact, provided unconsciously by the user. These answers may, however, contain information he did not know he possessed; they are provided by intuitive and telepathic processes well below the level of consciousness.

In glancing at the use of talismans as pendulums I may seem to digress from my main subject. The talismanic pendulum, however, does tell us something about talismans. Firstly, it suggests that talismans can act as an expression and transmitter of intuitive powers and perceptions of which we are unconscious. Secondly, it suggests that it is the human psyche which energizes the talisman in many cases, for the pendulum does not work unless it is held up by a human hand; if it is hung from an inanimate object it does not move. Thirdly, because of the way in which the user's belief about it can alter its movement, it indicates that its powers may be partially controlled by our view of its symbolic meaning. It is, indeed, important to understand the symbolism of the talisman one finds and possesses—the finder of a talismanic object needs to know something about traditional talismanic symbolism. He needs to be able to interpret at least something of the message he is receiving, to understand something of the nature of the sympathetic connection he feels. This connection may exist in terms of entirely personal obsessions, but may relate to traditional talismanic thinking of an intuitive nature. On the other hand the symbolism may only be explicable in terms of one of occult systems whose symbols appear to speak directly to the deep mind and which have done so effectively for hundreds of years.

Chapter 4

Traditional Talismans

> *Then I asked: "Does a firm persuasion that a thing is so, make it so?" He replied: "All Poets believe that it does, and in ages of imagination this form of persuasion removed mountains . . ."*
>
> William Blake[1]

Manufactured talismans are distinct from organic and found talismans, and they were common in all civilizations. They were intended to give protection against ill fortune of all kinds, some being more specific in intent than others. It was widely believed that all misfortune, or at least a substantial portion of all misfortune, was caused by psychic influences—those of demons, devils, dark angels, ill-wishing shamans, witch-doctors, or witches. While this may now strike many as somewhat melodramatic, we do know that just as we can inflict diseases upon ourselves psychosomatically, so others can affect us by the telepathic messages they send and by directing psychic energies towards us. That psychic energy can be used to affect actuality has been shown over and over again by experiments in psychokinesis in which a person, simply by concentration of the will, can move an object from one place to another. The evidence for psychokinetic power is considerable.

The form of psychic attack that most talismans were generally regarded as countering can be summed up simply in the

---

[1] *The Poetry and Prose of William Blake*, "The Marriage of Heaven and Hell," edited by David V. Erdman, Doubleday, New York, 1965, pp. 37-38.

phrase "the evil eye." The evil eye is a term for ill wishing by some particular person or persons. Many people in rural communities in Europe were believed to have the evil eye simply because they had a peculiarly intent gaze or a squint. They were often ostracized, sometimes beaten, and, in time of general misfortune, frequently killed. The evil eye was, it was believed, used equally against people, domestic beasts, and vegetables. If a man fell sick, or a cow ceased giving milk, or the butter would not come, or the apple tree failed to fruit, these disasters were likely to be blamed on the "evil eye" of some ill-wisher. There are more spells against the evil eye in the various collections of verbal magic than there are of any other kind.

While the evil eye is not the only kind of psychic attack, it seems to be the most universally recognized. Many societies have names for it: the Sumerian word was *Igi-Hul* (eye-evil); the Arabs call it *Ain al-hasad* (if they wish to avoid drawing its attention to themselves they refer to it as *Ain al-Jamal,* the eye of beauty); the Copts called it *Bon*, the Ethiopians *Ayenat,* the Greeks *Baskanos,* the Syrians *aina bisha,* the Armenians *paterak*. In Europe today it is called *bose Blick* in Germany, *booze blik* in the Netherlands, *Mal de ojo* in Spain, *innocchiatura* in Corsica, *mauvais oeil* in France, *droch-shuil* in Ireland, *szemverses* in Hungary, *skjoertunge* in Norway—the list is vast.

Belief in the evil eye was, of course, no more than a recognition of the power of psychic energy, combined with a belief that any disruption of normally harmonious existence must have

Figure 4.1 Hand of Fatima.

been caused by some malign person or spirit. The ability of shamans and witch doctors to detect the presence of a malign influence, to deduce its source, and to counter it with magical rituals and blessings made them important and powerful members of their communities. It was, however, necessary not only to counter an evil activity already in progress, but also to provide people with means to prevent such attacks. Thus the shamans and the witch doctors provided protective talismans, as well as talismans that conferred blessings. As time went by some talismans became generally accepted as effective in themselves and the shaman or witch doctor was not required to provide them. The cross became such a talisman for Christians, as did the cornu for Italians.

Several otherwise quite different social groups and magico-religious traditions have talismans in common. One instance of this is the talisman generally known as the Hand of Fatima (see Figure 4.1). This image of an open hand can be found among Egyptian talismans where it is regarded as a symbol of open heartedness and generosity, and as a protection against envy and all evil arising from emotions akin to envy. The Etruscans considered it symbolic of justice and victory. Sometimes combined with other images, such as an eye or other powerful symbol in the palm, the Hand of Fatima is a protection against envy or the evil eye.

The Mohammedans gave this talisman its name. Fatima was the Prophet's daughter by his first wife, Khadijah. She married Mohammed's cousin Ali, and bore him three sons, Hasan, Husain, and Muhain. Even after having these children she was called Virgin or Clean Maid *(Al-Batul)* and was also called by one of the names for Venus, *Al-Zahra.* This talisman is regarded as symbolizing Mohammed's family, the thumb being Mohammed himself, the first finger Fatima, the second finger Ali, and the last two Hasan and Husain. It therefore carries an enormous power for good. It also symbolizes the five main duties of Mohammedans: to observe the fast of Ramadan, to make a pilgrimage to Mecca, to give alms, to practice all the rites of ablution, and to be an enemy to infidels. The Hand of Fatima should, according to some authorities, be made of pottery or bronze, though the association with Venus might suggest that copper would be more appropriate. In modern times, however, it is usually made out of silver or a base metal or alloy of a silver color.

Figure 4.2 The Egyptian talisman of the *udjat* (eye).

The Mohammedans use another hand talisman which is made out of blue glass, one finger extended. It is hung around the necks of children to protect them from evil. An Etruscan hand amulet shows the hand closed with the thumb placed between the second and third fingers; worn as a pendant with the thumb pointing down it protects the wearer from the evil eye, as also does the talisman of the cornu, or horns, in which the hand is closed save for the first and last fingers which are extended. This talisman is used as a highly insulting gesture today in Italy. Another variety is an Egyptian amulet made simply of two straight fingers; this brings the wearer strength and power.

The hand amulet is typical in being not only attached, at one stage in its history, to a particular set of religious beliefs, but also in being accepted and trusted outside that system of beliefs. The talisman of the eye is similar in this. The Egyptian talisman of the *udjat* (Figure 4.2), which means simply eye, provided defense against

Figure 4.3 The Scarab. An Egyptian talisman used for general protective purposes.

the evil eye and provided its wearer with good health and physical protection. The *udjat* is the eye of Ra the sun god, which according to legend was once blinded by the evil powers during an eclipse, its sight being restored by Thoth. The Eye of Ra is sometimes combined with a second *udjat,* the eye of Aah the moon god, to form the *Udjatti,* a talisman in whose presence no evil person or thing can have power. The Eye of Ra is only one of many eyes to be found throughout the world. An eye is frequently painted on the prows of boats, in order to ensure successful navigation, as the eye symbolizes being able to see the way. In the middle east, an eye talisman is sometimes placed over the left eye of a horse to protect it from harm.

Another Egyptian talisman used for general protective purposes is the scarab (see Figure 4.3). This beetle collects dung, then lays an egg in it and molds it into a ball which it then pushes into a sunny place where the heat will hatch the egg. It symbolizes the god of creation rolling the ball of the sun across the sky. The model of the beetle, the scarab, is therefore a talisman not only to protect the wearer against evil but also to give him vitality and strength, the energy and drive of the god of creation. The Egyptians made scarabs of all sizes and of almost all materials, creating statues as well as talismanic rings, brooches and pendants, but the favorite materials were green stone and black basalt.

An insect talisman that may be derived from the scarab is that of a ladybird, which protects against poverty and indeed is supposed to bring wealth. It is traditionally made of gold, but there are many made of other metals. In Germany, the ladybird is associated with the Virgin Mary and called *Mariankafer.* In other places it is also called "God Almighty's Cow." It is thus associated with ideas of creation and bringing to life.

Talismans in the shapes of both insects and animals are very widespread. The Etruscans believed that a spider talisman brought wisdom, foresight, and riches. The Burmese believe that frog talismans can protect children from evil; the Egyptians considered them talismans for fruitfulness. In Chinese tradition, images of the stork and the crane bring health and long life, those of two bats ensure good fortune, and that of a goose domestic happiness. The image of the phoenix in China is believed to bring longevity and marital happiness, while in Japan it is supposed to endow the wearer with the virtues of rectitude, fidelity, and obedience to divine law. The Egyptians used a talisman of a vulture to prevent scorpion bites. The Chinese regarded the tortoise talisman as a protection against black magic and a bringer of health and long life.

Whether or not one understands or shares the religious beliefs of these various countries and peoples, a great many of their talismanic images still impress us. They appear to carry with them a kind of power accumulated from centuries of belief. It is as if our deep minds have been in some way conditioned to accept them. Once we know that a pretty little beetle badge has been, in the past, an object of religious importance, and that many millions of people have regarded it with awe, we tend to regard it with awe also. Once we view anything with awe, we admit the possibility that it has magical power, that it transmits messages, and the objects will have an effect on us and for us.

It is perhaps because the traditional symbol can be easily understood in terms of a powerful message and wondered at as something that has played an important part in many human lives that it is more effective as a talisman than many more recent creations. Moreover, many of these Traditional symbols are still a part of our lives and have meaning for us in contemporary terms as well as in terms of ancient beliefs. Such talismans are those of the heart, the key and the knot.

The heart talisman is of great antiquity. The Egyptians called it the *Ab* and it symbolized the vital power of the person, perhaps the power of the unconscious and immortality. Shown

Figure 4.4 The *Ab*. This heart-shaped talisman symbolized the vital power of the person.

as Figure 4.4, it was usually made of some red stone such as jasper, or of red glass, porcelain, wax, or paste. Later societies accepted it as symbolic of the vital force of life, but gradually it developed a more limited popular significance as symbolic of love, affection, and passion. Because it gives the wearer a constant sense of the power and importance of love, it protects him against hatred. It is also, of course, used as a love talisman in an active sense. Modern heart talismans are usually made of gold.

The key has been used as a talisman ever since keys came into being. The Greeks regarded the key image as a powerful talisman symbolizing knowledge, and possessing the ability to open a door to the unknown. The key was sacred to Apollo and Diana. The Romans, who thought it sacred to Janus and Jana, believed it effective in promoting prudence, memory of the past, and perception of the future, as well as ease in childbirth. The Japanese have a talisman of three keys, the keys of the granary, which brings the wearer happiness, riches, and love. In other countries the three keys are said to ensure love, wealth, and health. The emblem of Saint Peter is two crossed keys, and Saint Zita, the patron saint of domestic servants, has a bunch of keys as her device.

The key has appeared in different guises in many societies. Figure 4.5 on page 44 shows the Egyptian Ankh, which is formed of a letter T, or Tau, with a loop above the cross piece; it has been called "the key of life," and is a powerful protective amulet. Although in the first century A.D. it was placed alongside the Christian cross on tombs, it is not truly a cross, although some people have said it is a cross with a handle, a *crux ansata.* Others have believed it to represent a gibbet and yet others the hammer of Thor. Some believe it to be a representation of a phallus, which seems not unlikely, for it is clear that it symbolized the life force itself; all the Egyptian gods are seen carrying it in their right hands and presenting it to those who serve them. Indeed, some pictures show a god putting it to the nostrils of a corpse in order to awaken the dead to life. Another view is that the loop represents the open mouth of a fish giving birth to the waters of the Nile and therefore to life itself. Used as the symbol of Venus, the Ankh has also been said to symbolize the triumph of spirit (the loop or circle) over matter (the Tau cross). The Ankh is not only generally protective, therefore,

Figure 4.5 The Egyptian *Ankh*.

but also brings the wearer long life. It is interesting to note that it has come back into favor in the twentieth century and is now one of the most popular pendants in existence.

Because of its loop, the Ankh may be related to the talismanic knot. The knot was also an Egyptian talisman, and it has been used in many forms by many people from antiquity to the present. It is, of course, a symbol of that which joins and unifies, and is common in the form of lovers' knots which symbolize the joining of two people. It is also a protection, therefore, against the disruption of relationships, and a talisman to preserve the *status quo;* something that the talisman owner or maker has "tied" into the knot will also be preserved. In India and Tibet the knot talisman is protective against evil, for it is believed to secure the good forces and bind them together, and to provide a hindrance to the evil ones. Knot talismans are used in weddings, both in China and elsewhere for the above reason. A person at death's door, however, must have no knots upon him, as they will prevent the departure of the spirit.

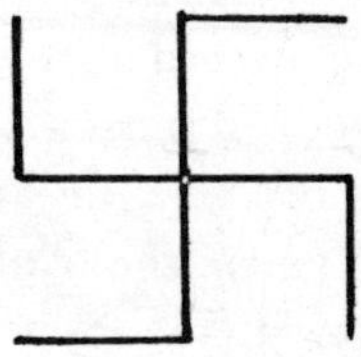

Figure 4.6 The swastika, gammadion or fylfot.

Similarly, knots in the clothing of a woman in labor may prevent the coming of the child.

Not all talisman retain their original symbolic meanings, or remain generally acceptable. Some become trivialized by popular misunderstandings; some fall victim to commerce and are recognized only as trademarks; some become so closely associated with particular social groups or sects as to lose their general universal meanings. One of the most ancient and powerful talismans, the swastika, has been affected in this way.

The swastika originated in ancient India. It is a cross, all of whose arms are of equal length, and made of "L" signs reversed, so that the ends of the arms all point to the right and suggest a clockwise spinning motion. This symbol, shown as Figure 4.6, is also known as the *gammadion* because the "L" reversed can also be read as the Greek letter *gamma.* It has also been known as the *fylfot,* which is a term taken from ancient designs for windows in which the symbol was used. A French term for it is *croix-pattee.* The *fylfot* sometimes exists in reversed form, which is to say that the arms point in a counterclockwise direction. This counterclockwise form is properly a *sauvastika* (see Figure 4.7).

The swastika has been interpreted in many different ways by commentators. Some have believed it to be a fire symbol portraying the crossing of two fire-sticks. Some have taken the swastika to represent the springtime sun, and the sauvastika the sun in autumn. Some think that it symbolizes the four quarters of the heaven or the four quarters of the earth. Others have seen it as the symbol of Indra, or Zeus, or Thor, or summed them all up in one and called it the symbol of the Supreme God. In general, it is accepted because of the wheel-like appearance, as a symbol both of the sun and of the Supreme Being, and as a good luck symbol.

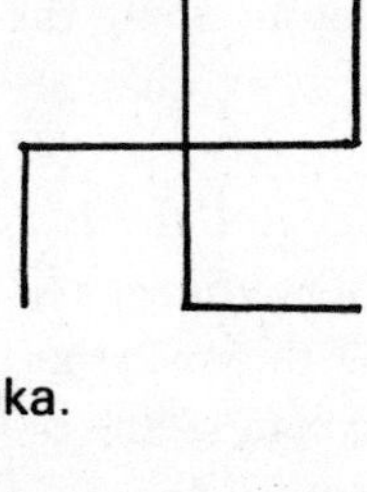

Figure 4.7 The Sauvastika.

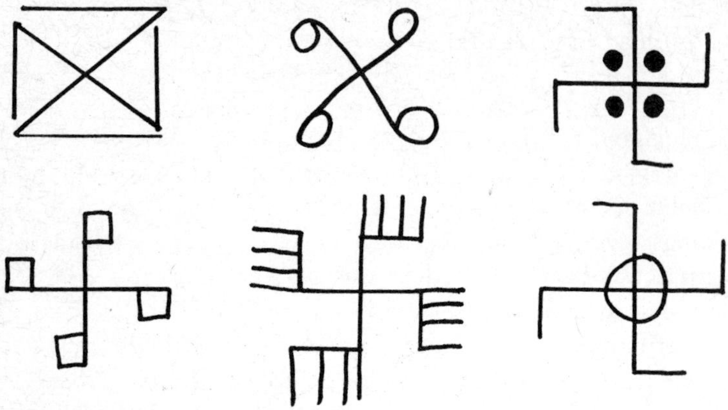

Figure 4.8 Some variations of the Sauvastika.

The symbol itself appears with some variation in many civilizations. (See Figure 4.8.) A Scythian swastika has little squares, like flags, tucked onto the ends of the arms. Another version turns the short parts of the arms into circles. On pottery, the sauvastika appears with four dots added, one in each of the angles made by the crossing of the arms at the center. It appears as a symbol of the Buddha on many statues and is also shown adorning the breast of Bodhisattvas. The Chinese name for the swastika is "thunderscroll" *(Lei-wen),* and when used as a written character means not only good luck, but prosperity and long life. In Sanskrit it means "purveyor of good fortune or well being." It is also known as the Wheel of the Law, and taken to represent both the cycle of the seasons and the human cycle of death and rebirth.

The swastika was used as an emblem by the Nazis in Germany; since it is an ancient Aryan symbol, it was therefore appropriate to the Nazi insistence upon what they chose to call Aryanism. It was also recognized by them as a power symbol. The Nazis caused the swastika to change in symbolism—it is now associated in our minds with so much tyranny, cruelty, and evil that many of us cannot get beyond these associations to the real and timeless significance of the symbol itself.

What happened to the swastika has happened to different effect, with the cross. The sign of the cross predates Christianity by many thousands of years, and it may even be the oldest talismanic symbol in the world. In the earliest known examples, the arms are all of equal length and at right angles to each other; this is known as the Greek or equilateral cross shown in Figure 4.9. It is clear, however, that the cross itself, and usually a form of equilateral cross, was a meaningful and potent symbol to mankind long before the days of Greek civilization. The cross has been interpreted as symbolizing the four quarters of heaven, and therefore, as a symbol of the power of the heavens and especially of the sun. Columbus was astonished to find it in America. It appears on many ancient Mexican and Peruvian artefacts and experts say that there it symbolized the four directions of the wind.

The cross on which Christ was crucified was probably one in which the horizontal arm was shorter than the vertical one and placed above the center of the vertical. Figure 4.10 on page 48 shows this cross, the Latin Cross (crux immissa or crux capitata) which has become the commonest form of the cross talisman. There are however other versions, such as those in Figure 4.11: the Cross of Lorraine, which has two cross pieces, the higher one being shorter than the lower, and an oriental version which adds a third short cross piece to the Cross of Lorraine near the foot of the vertical. There is also Saint Andrew's Cross which is in the form of an X (the crux decussada), and the Tau cross (or crux commissa), which is really not a cross at all, but the letter T or Greek Tau.

The cross did not become inextricably attached to Christianity until the fourth century when the Empress Helena is popularly supposed to have discovered the true cross. Thereafter, it became a sign of great protective power for Christians, and was re-adopted, or revived, as a talismanic sign by many non-Christians also. The

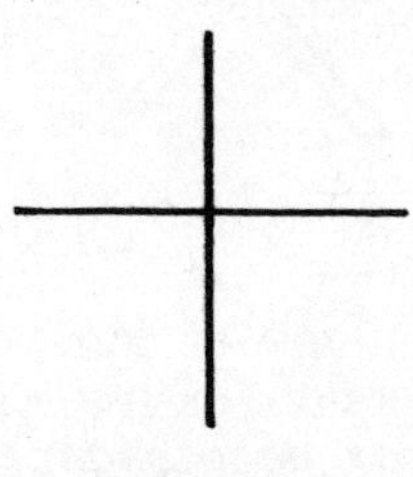

Figure 4.9 Greek or Equilateral Cross.

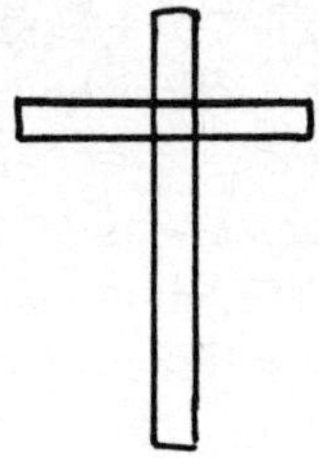

Figure 4.10 The Latin Cross *(crux immissa* or *crux capitata).*

Latin cross is now regarded as essentially Christian, but other forms of the cross are used without specific religious significance as powerful talismans against evil, and talismans of supreme power. It's interesting to note how Saint Andrew's Cross is used to "cross out" errors, which is to say to cancel and to defend against wrongs. The crossroads are, in all civilizations, regarded as places of magical power. The Romans even had a goddess of the crossroads called *Trivia.* Suicides are often buried at crossroads where their spirits are prevented by the sign of the cross from wandering from that place. Gallows were often erected at crossroads. The widespread notion that crossroads are haunted by evil spirits owes more to these practices than to any feeling that the sign of the cross is itself malign. Money is sometimes cached at crossroads, for there the cross will protect the treasure. In the Western world the sign for the kiss of love is a St. Andrew's cross. In folklore, before the advent of mechanical street cleaners, "there existed a profession of

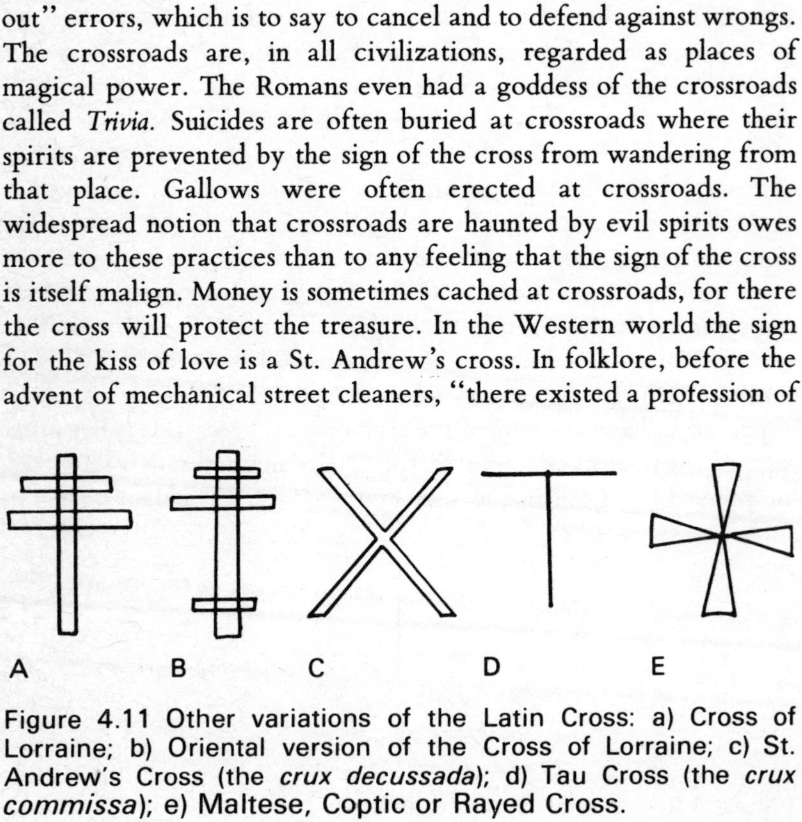

Figure 4.11 Other variations of the Latin Cross: a) Cross of Lorraine; b) Oriental version of the Cross of Lorraine; c) St. Andrew's Cross (the *crux decussada*); d) Tau Cross (the *crux commissa*); e) Maltese, Coptic or Rayed Cross.

crossing sweepers"—they, like chimney sweeps, were regarded as lucky people to meet. Crossing one's fingers is a talismanic gesture against misfortune, as of course is making the sign of the cross. People who are unable to write make a cross as their signature on documents. The cross, indeed, remains a powerful talisman even though one form of it has, like the swastika, become attached to a particular group of people.

The cross is regarded as a sun symbol, and, like all sun symbols, as a powerful protection against evil. Moon symbols are equally protective. The symbol of the crescent moon in its first quarter, which is to say with the horns of the moon pointing to the left, is a talisman against misfortune and the evil eye. (It is important to have the horns pointing left for this shows the moon on the increase and therefore is also a symbol of growing prosperity. Crescents pointing the other way portray a waning moon and are negative in effect.) The crescent was known as the *Saharon* by the Hebrews and was worn by women, presumably because of its fertility inducing powers, and by kings, because the king stands for the country and the country must be fertile. It was also tied around camels' necks as a protection against the evil eye.

Another ancient talismanic symbol is the mandala, shown in Figure 4.12 on page 50. In its most simple form it is a circle divided into four quarters by a cross, and it symbolizes unity and wholeness. The four segments may be read as thought, intuition, feeling and sensation; they may also be read as the four quarters of the heavens, the directions of the winds, and so forth. This basic form has been used to create extremely elaborate symbolic figures, some for aids to meditation and some as protective talismans. Frequently these talismans have a representation of the sun, which is the center of the universe, the all powerful god, and the human heart, at the middle of the design. Sometimes the circle includes a square which symbolizes the conscious controlling and ordering of the unity presented. All mandalas are protective.

In Figure 4.13 we see another mandalan talisman, the Chinese talisman of the Yang and Yin. It presents the unity of the universe and of the self in terms of the complementary interlocking of the feminine and the masculine, the dark and the light, night and day, above and below, in a form which also suggests, like the

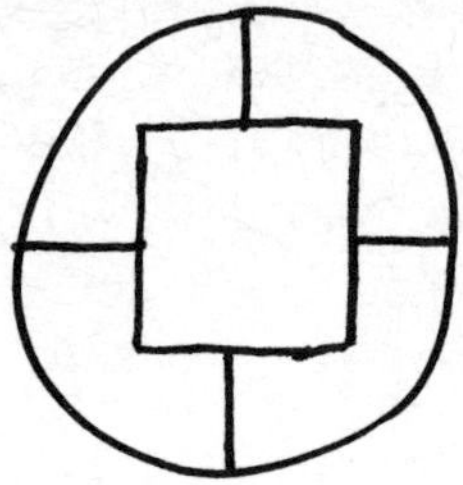

Figure 4.12 The Mandala (very simple form).

swastika, the turning wheel. This, again, is used as much for meditative as talismanic purposes, and is a wholly protective symbol.

The two most widely used talismanic signs are of course the five pointed star which is also known as the pentacle or pentagram, and the hexagon or hexagram. The pentacle (Figure 4.14) is also called the Seal of Solomon because, together with other signs, it is supposed to have been engraved on his signet ring. It is, however, of great antiquity and was found on Babylonian vessels long before the time of Solomon. It has been called the Pentalpha by the Greeks, and in the Middle Ages was sometimes referred to as the Goblins cross. It should be made with one stroke of the pen, brush, or engraving tool. If it is made of metal it should be made of one unbroken strip with only the one join to complete it. With the single point at the top it is a talisman against many evils; with the single point at the bottom it is an unfavorable talisman. It has been seen as representing the interlocking of the male and female principles, the five senses, the five books of Moses and of God. It is sometimes worn by travelers to ensure a successful return home or

Figure 4.13 The Yin and Yang.

Figure 4.14 The Pentagram.

as a talisman against the evil eye and demons. This is in its simplest form, unadorned by letters and other signs. It can be used in combination with other inscriptions such as names of angels, the signs of the zodiac and of the planets, and the names of God for more specific purposes.

Figure 4.15 shows an almost equally common talismanic sign, the hexagram, or six pointed star, which should be made of one piece of material, or with one stroke of the pen. This figure has been called the Shield of Solomon, and like the pentagram, has many uses when inscribed in various ways. A talisman against fire, for example, is a hexagram inscribed in the middle with AGLA, the initial letters of the four Hebrew words that spell out "Thou art mighty forever, Adonai," and the short and long versions of the name of God (YH and YHWH) written round the sides. Finally, a text from *Numbers 11:2* is inscribed on the reverse in such a way as to form a triangle—the top of the page is the base of the triangle, so that if read from right to left and downwards the message dwindles as, presumably, the power of the fire will dwindle.

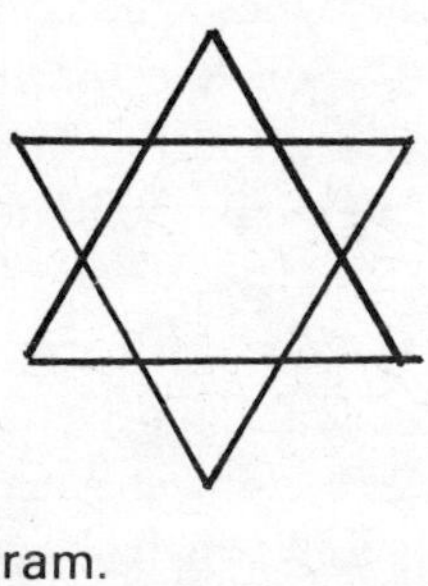

Figure 4.15 The Hexagram.

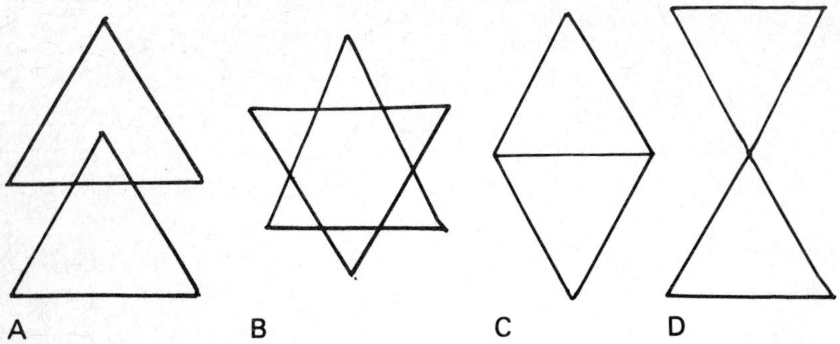

Figure 4.16 Hexagrams of the Elements: a) fire; b) earth; c) air; d) water.

Pentagrams and hexagrams have been used as protective talismans for centuries, and also as the ground plan for other talismans. Some practitioners of ceremonial magic make use of variations on the hexagram form to symoblize the four elements of Fire, Air, Water, and Earth. (See Figure 4.16.)

The symbol of the fish has been used as a talisman for many centuries, and was used as a badge by the early Christians. The derivation for this use comes from the Greek word for fish, *ichthus,* which is also an acronym for the Greek phrase *Iesous Christos, Theou Uios Soter* ("Jesus Christ, the Son of God the Savior"). Both before and after the birth of Christianity, however, it was regarded as a talisman of good fortune that protects from poverty, and promotes fertility and riches.

The Egyptians also considered the fish to be a talisman to bring abundance, wealth, and domestic happiness because the fish was the symbol of the god Hathor who controlled the waters of the Nile. The fish as a god—Dagon, the sun fish—was worshipped by the Syrians. The Egyptians revered the Abtu fish and the Ant fish—they were believed to protect the boat in which Ra the Sun God sails by swimming beside it to drive away evil. Some talismans show the Christian cross with two fish swimming beside it, thus combining both Christian and Egyptian symbolism.

The fish is one of the eight emblems of Buddhism; the god Vishnu's first incarnation took this form, and the fish talisman is considered to bring wealth. The Romans regarded the fish talisman as a protection against colic, dropsy, and other "watery" diseases. The fish is associated with Venus, whose day is Friday, and members of the Catholic Church are required to abstain from meat and eat fish on this day. In general, the fish talisman is a protective talisman associated with the bringing of prosperity and fertility and with the power of the sun or supreme being.

The talisman of the scorpion is a powerful protection against an enemy, and can also be used as an active talisman to destroy an ill wisher. Arrowheads and axes are also protective against ill wishers.

Most of the above talismans are visual representations. Not all talismans are of this kind. Fringed clothing has been worn in many societies to avert the influence of evil spirits. Bells sewn to garments have the same function; the Romans used to attach rattles to the garments of their children. Some societies have used jangling bracelets and anklets for the same reason. These are often worn during ritual dances, as are the anklets made of deer hooves of the Haida and Kwakiutl Indians. The bells attached to the clothes of the Morris dancers in Britain, and the bell attached to the hobby horse of the professional jester, probably had originally the same functions as do the coins sewn on gypsies clothing, and the pearl buttons on the outfits of London costermongers or "pearlies." Bells and noisemakers everywhere are regarded as having talismanic and protective properties. The Chinese use firecrackers to keep off evil spirits. Other societies have used gongs, drums, and wind instruments. These are talismanic rather than true talismans in that it is the sound which does the work and the power does not reside in the objects themselves. Nevertheless, by association bells have come to be regarded in themselves as talismans; many of them are inscribed with the swastika to make their protective influence even more certain, even in Christian churches.

Other manufactured talismans have more specific protective qualities. In the Punjab one wears copper rings, bracelets, or earrings as a protection against rheumatism and sciatica, and in the western world copper is regarded as a defense against rheumatism. Rings of iron are worn or carried in both India and the western world as a protection against witchcraft. According to western folklore, witches of evil disposition are repelled by cold iron. The

Chinese protect their children from misfortune by making them wear bracelets and anklets of jade. Jade rings have become popular once again in the twentieth century in the West, though only a few wearers know the talismanic reason for wearing them.

Many manufactured talismans are simply metal models of natural objects which have been long regarded as having talismanic power, or of objects which are too clumsy or awkward to wear in themselves. Thus there are more models of horseshoes worn for good fortune than there are real horseshoes, and metal models of rabbit's feet are more commonly carried than rabbit's feet themselves. The vast majority of traditional talismanic symbols, however, appear to relate to some central mystery of existence, and to attitudes and beliefs which form a part of almost all religious systems. Many of them, such as the cross and the heart, go back thousands of years, and appear to derive their power from the symbolic language in which they speak to the deep mind, and from the awe with which we regard objects that have been venerated in one way or another for many centuries. It also seems true that any talisman which has passed through the hands of many people, all of whom have used its talismanic powers, has gathered a powerful energy field, and will therefore be more effective than one of modern manufacture. The age of talismans is always a matter of interest to those who seek them out; the older they are the more credible they are felt to be and, therefore, the more powerful.

Not all talismans make their appeal only to the deep mind. Those Egyptians who wore the scarab and the ankh, and those Babylonians who inscribed the cross and the swastika on their pottery, were consciously aware of the place these symbols had in their religious beliefs; conscious understanding of the symbolism helps to direct the deep mind, of course, for conscious and intuitive response are then combined. This is especially the case with talismans made in the figures of the gods. These are extremely numerous, for they occur in all cultures and societies, and it would require a book in itself to list even half of them. Perhaps here it is only necessary to say that all the images of Indian, Chinese, Japanese, and other gods that can be seen in stores devoted to antiques and curios are talismanic, and that if you purchase one you should look up its significance in a book on the religion and mythology of the country concerned. The appearance of the god is often of little help. Many that look ferocious are benevolent; some that appear to be harmless have harmful uses. Who would suppose that the Ganesa, the elephant-headed god of India, were a god of wisdom and literature, and, as a talisman, powerful in the removal of obstacles and difficulties and of great help when beginning important business? Who would think that Hanuman, the monkey god, were a powerful good fortune talisman? These talismans are indeed difficult to understand at first glance, as are all esoteric visual symbols.

Chapter 5

Talismanic Stones

When the soul of the world, by its virtue, does make all things (that are generated or artificially made) fruitful, by sealing and impressing on them Celestial Virtues for the work of some wonderful effect, then things themselves . . . when they are conveniently bound to, or wrapped up, or suspended about the neck, or any other way applied, although by ever so easy a contract, they do impress their virtue upon us.

Albertus Magnus:
Egyptian Secrets

From time immemorial, talismans have been made from precious and semi-precious stones, and there is a considerable amount of lore connected with them. Some of this is purely medical lore, involving the stone being crushed into powder or burned in the fire and eaten.[1] There are other medical uses for stones which are talismanic, such as the laying of particular stones upon different parts of the body to cure illness, or the holding of stones in the hand when sick, or the dipping of stones in water or wine which is afterwards drunk. Most talismans are worn on the body and often next to the skin, and many people believe that no talisman can be effective unless it is in contact with their bodies. Therefore, the dipping of a stone or any other talisman in water may be thought of as the transference of some power or virtue from the talisman

[1]Practices which involve the alteration of the stone from its original state do not concern us here, since this chapter will address talismanic uses of unaltered stone.

proper into a medicine. Some stones are regarded as having medical properties which may or may not be truly talismanic, and these are often carved into goblets from which wine or water may be drunk. There is a gray area here, as no real distinction was made by the early users of talismans, or indeed by early medical practitioners, between psychic and physical operations. Some cures which we now know to be based upon the physical properties of plants and herbs were regarded as being just as magical as the cures we now regard as entirely psychic or psychological. These days, the world of medicine is slowly coming around to the views of its forebears in that the doctors are no longer regarding psychological and psychic methods of healing as outside the province of medicine proper.

Precious and semi-precious stones are also effective curative talismans because of the shapes into which they have been cut or carved—certain shapes can contain, resonate, and transmit energy in the same way as the pyramid. The interesting phenomenon of "pyramid power" has shown us that blunt razor blades, when placed under cardboard replicas of the Cheops pyramid and oriented, in the same way, north to south, will regain their edge. It has also been shown that the pyramid will keep meat fresh, aid in the healthy growth of plants, and if suspended over a bed, will help sick people to sleep and assist the healing process. Pyramids are now in use at several hospitals.[2] It is apparently not the material of the pyramid that matters, but the pyramid's shape. This would go some way towards explaining why cut diamonds and crystals of all kinds are considered powerful talismans. Of course, the properties of crystals are well known to science, and crystals are used in many ways by technology. We may, therefore, in listing talismanic stones and especially precious stones, be touching upon something which may, like so many "magical" beliefs of the past, come to be explored and understood in terms of physical properties.

In addition to their medical properties, talismans made of precious and semi-precious stones in various combinations have been popular for centuries. Perhaps the most famous one of these is Aaron's Breastplate, which was to be worn as a talismanic aid to

---

[2]For a more in-depth discussion of the medical uses of pyramids, readers should see Lyle Watson's fascinating book, *Supernature*, Bantam Books, New York, 1974.

making correct judgments in disputes. It is described in *Exodus 28: 15-21:*

> *And thou shalt make the breastplate of judgement with cunning work.....of gold, of blue, and of purple, and of scarlet, and of fine twisted linen, shalt thou make it.*
>
> *Foursquare it shall be, being doubled; a span shall be the length thereof, and a span shall be the breadth thereof.*
>
> *And thou shalt set in it settings of stones, even four rows of stones: the first row shall be a sardius, a topaz, and a carbuncle: this shall be the first row.*
>
> *And the second row shall be an emerald, a sapphire, and a diamond.*
>
> *And the third row a ligure, an agate, and an amethyst.*
>
> *And the fourth row a beryl, and an onyx, and a jasper; they shall be set in gold in their inclosings.*
>
> *And the stones shall be with the names of the children of Israel, twelve according to their names, like the engravings of a signet; every one with his name shall they be according to the twelve tribes.*[3]

The New English Bible gives the stones as First Row: sardin, chrysolite and green feldspar. Second Row: purple garnet, lapis lazuli, jade. Third Row: turquoise, agate, jasper. Fourth Row: topaz, cornelian, green jasper. This version states also that the stones should be set in rosettes made of gold.

Talismanic stones are regarded as having power in themselves, but when they are mounted in brooches, formed into pendants, or set in rings their power is frequently increased by means of inscriptions. These inscriptions may simply spell out the particular one of their attributes that the wearer wishes to emphasize and call into play. It may consist of the appropriate sign

---

[3]All quotations from the Bible are from the King James version unless otherwise stated.

of the zodiac. Many gems are inscribed, however, with symbols that have been significant to humanity for thousands of years, and a great many precious and semi-precious stones are used to create carved images which combine the power of the material used with the power of the symbol—we will look at the subject of inscribed talismans in the next chapter.

The following list presents precious and semi-precious stones, and their talismanic properties. Many stones are associated with planets, signs of the zodiac, and months, as these have special symbolic significance. These associations appear in parentheses after the name of the stone: I have used the currently accepted associations rather than the older and now disputed ones.

Agate (Gemini)

Black agate provides courage, prosperity, and success in games. *Red agate* protects the wearer from lightning, thunderbolts, and the bites of snakes and insects. *Tawny agate* has all the properties of black and red agate and also increases the wearer's intelligence, brings good fortune in love, protects against insanity and fever, and gives victory in battle. If held in the hand when one is ill, it will speed up recovery and make it certain. It also gives the wearer longevity. *Grey agate* cut into a triangular shape and worn as a pendant protects the wearer from indigestion, intestinal disorder, and stiffness of the neck. If a woman wishes to prevent herself ever becoming sterile she should drink water in which a *green agate* ring has been washed. *Black agate* with white veins strengthens the wearer's heart. *Moss agate* will help a man have a good harvest if he wears it on the upper part of his right arm and upon the right horn of each of his oxen. (This may be an instance of sympathetic magic, for the markings on moss agate look like the branches of trees and other vegetation.) It will also strengthen a man's eyesight. *All agates* were believed by the Persians to make men eloquent, to ease their fevers, to bring good fortune in the form of bequests and legacies, to help in the discovery of hidden treasure, and to increase amiability. The Greeks considered agates to bring health, wealth and long life.

Alum

Alum, if sewn into a person's clothing, protects against the evil eye. If placed at the threshold of a house it will give the house the same protection.

Amber (Leo)

Amber protects children against convulsions and being poisoned. If it is carved into the shape of a phallus it protects against the evil eye. When carved into the shapes of fish, frogs, lions, dogs, or hares, it makes men virile and women fertile. Amber beads are a protection against witchcraft and many illnesses, including rheumatism, toothache, migraine, and most diseases of the digestive system. An amber talisman will get rid of a goitre, prevent insanity, and ward off attacks of erysipelas and catarrh. The Chinese regard it as symbolic of courage.

Amethyst (Jupiter, Aquarius)

If this talisman is tied round the neck by means of the feathers of peacocks and swallows it protects against the evil eye. Wine drunk from goblets made of amethyst will not cause drunkenness. If placed under the pillow, an amethyst will bring enjoyable dreams and improve the memory. Amethysts bring their wearer peace of mind and amiability and prevent them from losing their tempers. Rings of amethyst should be worn on the third finger of the left hand. They bring the wearer shrewdness in business matters. Amethyst rings are worn as protection by lawyers, doctors, bishops, businessmen, and sailors. If an amethyst is engraved with the symbols of the sun and the moon it will protect the wearer from witchcraft, and from being poisoned. If cut in the shape of a heart and set in silver and used as a love-gift, it will bring happiness and good fortune to the couple concerned, for it is the stone of St. Valentine.

Aquamarine (Scorpio, October)

Aquamarine differs from beryl in that it is always green, whereas beryl ranges from blue to white. Aquamarine earrings bring the wearer friendship and love. The aquamarine symbolizes hope, health, and youthful vitality.

Beryl (Scorpio, October)

Beryl symbolizes hope and protects against the evil eye. It sharpens intelligence, cures laziness, and brings peace of mind. If it is carved in the shape of a frog or has a frog engraved on it, it makes peace between enemies and promotes friendship and marital love. It heals illnesses of the liver and stomach and eases soreness of the throat and pain in the jaws. It preserves sailors and travelers from danger and is useful in discovering anything hidden. If worn as a ring or a pendant it should be set in gold.

Bloodstone (Aries, March)

Bloodstone is a red speckled green chalcedony. Worn as a talisman, it prevents the wearer from being cheated or deceived and yet makes all the wearer's statements convincing. It heals discord, prevents melancholy, strengthens the stomach, prolongs life, and makes its wearer both rich and courageous. If dipped in water and placed on a wound it will help to heal it, and it will also assist in curing dropsy and the ague. When engraved with a scorpion it will prevent stones in the bladder. Some say it should be set in gold, others silver.

Carbuncle (Scorpio)

Carbuncle refers to a garnet or ruby or any deep red stone. It protects the wearer from nightmares, poison, plague, and incontinence. It brings increased energy as it stimulates the heart, and also brings determination and health. It protects children from drowning and soldiers from being killed in war. Carbuncles protect the wearer from extravagance and from being bewitched, and bring the possessor increased energy, confidence, and determination as well as popularity and good health. When hung around the neck a carbuncle will cure sore throats and indigestion. In Africa and the East it was believed to prevent soldiers being wounded in battle.

Cat's Eye (Cancer)

The cat's eye protects the wearer from being bewitched and ensures wealth and long life. It is a protection against death, and if a woman drinks milk in which a cat's eye has been washed, she can make love without fear of becoming pregnant. (It is not clear how long the effect lasts!) The Assyrians believed the cat's eye could confer invisibility. If hung around the neck it will relieve asthma and cure croup in babies. It promotes strength of mind and ensures success in games of chance and all business speculations.

Carnelian

Carnelian worn in a ring prevents the wearer from becoming melancholy and pessimistic and promotes friendship. It gives the wearer ease of mind and defends against the evil eye.

Chalcedony (Aries)

Chalcedony, when blue, is regarded as having the same qualities as sapphire. If engraved with a man on a horse holding a pike and galloping, it protects travelers. White chalcedony increases the flow of milk in nursing mothers. It also assists the wearer to become popular and to be victorious, drives away nightmares and protects in times of political and social upheaval. It cures melancholy and protects the wearer from the evil eye.

Chrysolite (Sun, Leo)

Chrysolite brings wisdom and prudence, and if engraved with an ass, protects the wearer from gout.

Chrysoprase (Gemini)

Chrysoprase brings its wearer joy.

Coral (Libra)

Coral talismans are not only worn, but also hung on doorposts, bedposts, and in the house. Coral of all colors, with the exception of brown, protects against the evil eye, witchcraft, nightmares and demons, and prevents sterility. *Brown coral,* however, attracts evil forces. *White coral*, like white chalcedony, improves the milk supply of nursing mothers. It protects against thunderstorms, lightning, and hail, and is a good luck talisman worn by many ballet dancers. *Red coral*, if engraved with a man carrying a sword, stops hemorrhages, promotes emotional attachments and is a defense against the plague. All coral except brown coral protects against colic, whooping cough, and convulsions in children, and in the East is believed to cure cholera. When tied to a ship's mast, coral prevents shipwreck and drives away storms. Tied to fruit trees it ensures a good harvest. Coral is said to change color in the presence of poison or when illness is imminent.

Diamond (Aries)

Diamonds were considered unlucky by some people until the sixteenth century, but since that time they have been very highly regarded. The diamond brings its wearer good fortune of all kinds, and the finer the stone the greater the fortune. Diamonds defend the wearer from all forms of evil, and promote sincerity, loyalty, affection, and candor. Worn on the left arm a diamond will keep off wild beasts and demons, promote courage, and give its wearer victory in battle. Worn as a pendant it protects against the evil eye and the plague. The diamond is an antidote to all poisons and also prevents nightmares. It strengthens both body and mind, and water into which it has been dipped preserves the drinker from gout and apoplexy. A necklace of green-tinted diamonds eases childbirth. If set in steel a diamond is a protection against insanity. However, care should be taken in how diamonds are used. Very large stones are believed to cause mental distress in the wearer, and cuff links and buttons made of diamonds are believed to bring ill fortune or even death. Diamonds, moreover, should always be given and never bought or sold. Stolen diamonds bring great misfortune to the thief. Diamonds that have been cut into square or triangular shapes make people quarrelsome and cause mental distress, although diamonds of other shapes, especially those with six corners, bring good fortune and improve the strength and vitality of the wearer in old age.

Emerald (Venus, Cancer)

Emeralds promote fidelity, especially in love relationships, and protect the wearer from the evil eye and from convulsions. They also assist the wearer both to remember the past and to foresee future events. Emeralds engraved with a starling help the eyesight. Constipation and loss of appetite may be cured by gazing at an emerald. Emerald talismans calm storms at sea, help people find things they have lost, promote eloquence, and bring wealth and strength. Emeralds worn as rings will grow hot when they are near poison, lose their color in the presence of treachery, and blind poisonous snakes. Ideally, emeralds should only be worn by those born under the sign of Cancer.

Feldspar (Cancer)

Feldspar protects the wearer against sunstroke, headaches, and nosebleeds.

Garnet (Saturn, Aquarius)

Garnets promote loyalty and devotion and increase energy, health, and good humour. They prevent the wearer from poison and the plague and lightning. They prevent bad dreams and diseases of the skin, and change color when danger threatens. If a garnet is engraved with a lion it will prevent epidemics and protect travelers.

Haematite

Haematite makes the wearer lively and sexually vital and also promotes success in legal matters. Rings bearing haematites cure internal bleeding, blood spots in the eyes and snake bites, and protect the wearer from sunstroke and migraine.

Heliotrope

(See Bloodstone, page 62.)

Hyacinth

(See Zircon, page 72.)

Jade (Virgo, September)

Jade, or *Nephrite*, varies in color. *White jade* cures diseases and discomfort of the intestines. *Black jade* brings the wearer increased strength. *Green jade* banishes wild animals and evil spirits, and cures palpitations. Jade held in the hand and gently rubbed when making an important decision of any kind will ensure that the decision leads to good fortune. All jade prevents epilepsy and ophthalmia, and also averts accidents and injuries. Worn as a necklace it cures disorders of the stomach and the kidney, and in Chinese tradition, when carved in the shapes of a bat or stork, promotes long life. Jade was highly prized by the ancient Chinese who regarded it as symbolizing the finest qualities of man: benevolence, the understanding of signs and symbols, righteousness, virtuous actions, purity, innocence, moral conduct, and, because when made into a gong or bell, it produces a very clear and sweet note, musical ability.

Jasper (Aries, March)

Jasper brings happiness and relieves pain, protects the wearer from demons and snake bites, and improves the quality and amount of a nursing mother's milk. It also fortifies women during pregnancy.

Jet (Capricorn, January)

Jet, being black, is worn as a token of mourning, but also protects against the evil eye, especially when carved in the shape of the *Mano cornata* or the scarab. It protects the wearer from snake bites, thunderstorms, epilepsy and convulsions, and black magic. It should not be worn by anyone born under the signs of Aries or Libra.[4]

Lapis Lazuli (Libra, October)

Lapis Lazuli increases the wearer's natural abilities and brings success. It prevents miscarriages, and, in the form of beads worn around the neck, is a protection against the evil eye and the dangers of traveling. It promotes chastity and brings the help of good spirits; it also helps cure disorders of the skin, the blood, and the spleen. Lapis Lazuli necklaces cure melancholy, inspire courage in children, bless friends with fidelity, and bring lovers success. Lapis lazuli is associated both with Venus and the Virgin Mary.

---

[4]This is a widely held belief for which I have no explanation.

Lodestone (Scorpio, November)

Lodestone, or magnetite, is neither a precious nor a semi-precious stone, but because it is a magnet and shows true north, it has always been regarded as a powerful talisman. It brings the wearer courage and invulnerability. If bound to the feet it will cure gout. Combined with coral in a necklace it eases childbirth. When combined with silver it sharpens the eyesight; when set in gold it brings strength to the heart. It loses its powers if placed next to diamonds or garlic, but it regains its strength when provided with iron filings or dipped in the blood of a goat. It brings the wearer health, vitality, and the love of both gods and men. Set in a wedding ring it ensures the success of the marriage.

Malachite (Capricorn, January)

Malachite prevents rheumatism, colic, and cholera, protects the wearer from lightning and contagious diseases, and ensures health and success. It promotes constancy of affection and sound sleep and, when engraved with the symbol of the sun, prevents melancholy. It is also a protection against the evil eye.

Moonstone (Pisces, Cancer)

Moonstones can be hung on trees to ensure a good yield of fruit and promote health and strength in plants. They protect the wearer from the evil eye, nervous disorders and convulsions. A moonstone will enable its possessor to foresee the future if held in the mouth on a night of the full moon. It should be engraved with the image of a swallow. It promotes reconciliation between lovers, and if worn during the waxing of the moon, it will ease tuberculosis. It prevents dropsy, protects travelers and vitalizes the imagination.

Onyx (Aquarius, Saturn, August, Capricorn)

Onyx is a stone whose talismanic properties are variously debated. According to some it prevents bad dreams, but others say it causes nightmares and premature childbirth. Still others maintain that it eases childbirth and protects the wearer from the evil eye by returning the evil vibrations to their source. Some maintain that it breaks up friendships, and is generally unlucky; others maintain that it vitalizes the imagination, brings spiritual power, and cures convulsions. All agree that onyx improves the wearer's perceptiveness. The *black onyx* is regarded as particularly powerful.

Opal (Scorpio, Libra)

The opal provides qualities of fidelity and spiritual assurance according to some, but others believe it to be capable of acting as an evil eye. Nevertheless, it is said to improve the health of the eyes and strengthen the memory and the intellect. Because it has many colors, some say that it has all the powers of other stones associated with those colors—the emerald, the ruby, the garnet, the amethyst and the carbuncle. *Black opals* are generally regarded as bringers of good fortune. The opal enables the wearer to see into the future, but if this ability is used selfishly it will result in misfortune, especially in love. Although opals may be given as tokens of friendship, they are unlucky when used in engagement rings. They should not be worn by anyone born under the signs of Cancer or Capricorn.

Pearl (Cancer)

The pearl reinforces moral purity and supports chastity. It also prevents attacks by sharks.

Pumice

Pumice helps to ease labor pains and ensures a satisfactory birth.

Peridot (Leo)

The Peridot, a deep green chrysolite, protects the wearer from being bewitched and banishes melancholy and delusions. It should be set in gold.

Ruby (Leo, Capricorn, Mars, December)

Ruby is now considered the birthstone of December though it was once regarded as that of July, and is associated with late Capricorn. It has also been associated with Taurus and Mars. It protects its owner's house from storm damage. It makes men invulnerable in battles, heals quarrels, mitigates the fury of lust, promotes love and friendship. It increases beauty in women and protects the wearer from witchcraft and from both the plague and starvation. It changes color in the presence of poison or danger. It prevents bad dreams and illness of the spleen and liver. The variety of ruby known as *Spinel* gives protection against hail and storm.

Sapphire (Taurus, Libra, April)

The sapphire is nowadays considered to be the birthstone of April and has to be associated with Taurus, though in the past it has been associated with Venus, Gemini, Mercury, Saturn, and Jupiter. Gazing at a sapphire improves the eyesight. It brings the wearer health, strength, and social success, and promotes chastity, innocence and truthfulness. It sharpens intelligence and enables the wearer to understand the most obscure and difficult statements. It protects the wearer from envy, fraud, and the evil eye. If the wearer happens to be imprisoned it will help him to be released. According to one source, Aaron's rod was made of sapphire. It should be engraved with a ram.

Sardonyx (Virgo, Leo)

Sardonyx improves vitality and brings fame. It protects the wearer from infectious diseases and the bites of snakes and insects, especially scorpions. Worn around the neck it will bring friendship, happiness in marriage, and a successful outcome to legal business. It will strengthen self-control, especially in those prone to dissipation, and protect the wearer from witchcraft. When engraved with an eagle or the figures of Mars or Hercules it makes the wearer courageous. It also eases the pains of childbirth. It should be set in gold.

Serpentine

Serpentine protects the wearer from poison and the bites of snakes and insects. A serpentine goblet will sweat if the drink within it is poisoned, but will improve the taste and potency of any non-toxic liquid it holds, especially medicine.

Topaz (Mars, Saturn, Sagittarius, November)

Topaz brings the wearer love and affection and improves the disposition. It should be engraved with the figure of a falcon. If it is worn on the left arm it protects against the evil eye. If worn on the breast it will prevent thirst. Worn on the left hand, it improves the wearer's intelligence and courage and protects from melancholy. It prevents the wearer from feeling envy, and assists in the curing of liver disorders. The *yellow topaz* ensures health and prevents sudden death. It makes the wearer cautious and wise, and helps the traveler avert danger. It protects the wearer from the effects of air pollution, and from scalds and burns. It has been considered a cure for gout, asthma, insomnia, hemorrhoids, and liver disorder. It calms anger, prevents sensual overindulgence, and brings wealth, happiness and the admiration of those in authority. It should not be worn by those born under the signs of Pisces and Virgo.

Tourmaline (Leo)

Tourmaline inspires the mind and brings friendship and good fortune.

Turquoise (Saturn, Mercury, Venus, Taurus, December)

Turquoise brings the wearer courage and promotes success in all endeavors. It is a powerful talisman against evil and a bringer of great good fortune. It grows moist and changes color in the presence of poison. It protects horsemen from falls and ensures that their mounts remain surefooted and do not tire. It protects the wearer from eye disease and from the bites of snakes and insects.

Zircon (Aquarius, Sun, January)

The most potent talismanic variety of zircon is the deep red or bright orange *hyacinth*, which is also known as *jacinth*. It promotes fidelity and protects the wearer from insomnia, melancholy, bad dreams, and evil spirits. It cures jealousy and suspiciousness, protects travelers from theft, eases childbirth, strengthens the heart, the muscles and digestion, and protects the wearer from the plague, contagious diseases, and all forms of injury. It protects the wearer against lightning strike, promotes prudence, and helps the wearer to be successful in business. The *white zircon* and the pink or yellow zircon, known as *jargoon*, have the same attributes, but to a lesser extent. Zircon should not be worn by anyone born under the signs of Taurus or Scorpio.

Chapter 6

Inscriptive Talismans

Whoso hath a copy of this in his house, no evil spirit nor evil shall vex him, nor hunger nor ague, nor any evil spirit shall annoy; but all goodness shall be where a copy of this shall be found.

From a 17th Century Inscriptive Talisman

So many talismans involve the engraving or writing of words and names of power that it is necessary to devote a separate chapter to talismans composed of inscriptions. The simplest form of inscriptive talisman is perhaps that which simply presents the name of the spiritual power whose protection one is seeking. In Mohammedanism there are ninety-nine names of God and each one has a distinct and separate meaning (see Table 6.1 on pages 76-78). In kabbalistic thought there are ten names of God which also have different significances (see Table 6.2 on page 79).

Talismans make use of other names than those of God, of course. There are a great many which utilize local deities, and the names of spirits associated with different powers. It is impossible to list all these here, but we can perhaps illustrate the situation by looking at one particular group.

A large number of Saints and Martyrs have been designated as Patron Saints, and talismans bearing their names and/or emblems are considered to be protective.[1] Some Saints have also been listed as appropriate powers to invoke when attempting to prevent or cure

---

[1] I have not attempted to list the patron saints of countries or cities as these are extremely numerous and frequently derived from dubious local traditions.

Table 6.1 The Ninety-nine Names of God (Mohammedan)

1.	Ar-Rahman	The Merciful
2.	Ar-Rahim	The Compassionate
3.	Al-Malik	The King
4.	Al-Kuddus	The Holy
5.	As-Salam	The Peace
6.	Al-Mu'min	The Faithful
7.	Al-Muhaimin	The Protector
8.	Al-'Aziz	The Mighty
9.	Al-Jabbar	The Repairer
10.	Al-Mutakabbir	The Great
11.	Al-Khalik	The Creator
12.	Al-Bari	The Maker
13.	Al-Musawwir	The Fashioner
14.	Al-Ghaffar	The Forgiver
15.	Al-Kahhar	The Dominant
16.	Al-Wahhab	The Bestower
17.	Al-Razzah	The Provider
18.	Al-Fattah	The Opener
19.	Al-Alim	The Knower
20.	Al-Kabiz	The Restrainer
21.	Al-Basit	The Spreader
22.	Al-Khafiz	The Abaser
23.	Ar-Rafi'	The Exalter
24.	Al-Mu'izz	The Honorer
25.	Al-Muzil	The Destroyer
26.	As-Sami'	The Hearer
27.	Al-Basir	The Seer
28.	Al-Hakim	The Ruler
29.	Al-'Adl	The Just
30.	Al-Latif	The Subtle
31.	Al-Khabir	The Aware
32.	Al-Halim	The Clement
33.	Al-'Azim	The Grand
34.	Al-Ghafur	The Forgiving
35.	Ash-Shakur	The Grateful
36.	Al-'Ali	The Exalted
37.	Al-Kabir	The Great
38.	Al-Hafiz	The Guardian
39.	Al-Mukit	The Strengthener

Table 6.1 The Ninety-nine Names of God (continued)

40. Al-Hasib	The Reckoner
41. Al-Jalil	The Majestic
42. Al-Karim	The Generous
43. Ar-Rakib	The Watcher
44. Al-Mujib	The Approver
45. Al-Wasi'	The Comprehensive
46. Al-Hakim	The Wise
47. Al-Wadud	The Loving
48. Al-Majid	The Glorious
49. Al-Bais	The Raiser
50. Ash-Shadid	The Witness
51. Al-Hakk	The Truth
52. Al-Wakil	The Advocate
53. Al-Kawi	The Strong
54. Al-Matin	The Firm
55. Al-Wali	The Patron
56. Al-Hamid	The Laudable
57. Al-Muhsi	The Counter
58. Al-Mubdi	The Beginner
59. Al-Mu'id	The Restorer
60. Al-Muhyi	The Quickener
61. Al-Mumit	The Killer
62. Al-Hayy	The Living
63. Al-Kaiyum	The Subsisting
64. Al-Wajid	The Finder
65. Al-Majid	The Glorious
66. Al-Wahid	The One
67. As-Samad	The Eternal
68. Al-Kadir	The Powerful
69. Al-Muktadir	The Prevailing
70. Al-Mukaddim	The Bringer Forward
71. Al-Mu'akhkhir	The Deferrer
72. Al-Awwal	The First
73. Al-Akhir	The Last
74. Az-Zahir	The Evident
75. Al-Batin	The Hidden
76. Al-Wali	The Governor
77. Al-Muta'ali	The Exalted
78. Al-Barr	The Righteous

Table 6.1 The Ninety-nine Names of God (continued)

79.	At-Tawwab	The Accepter of Repentance
80.	Al-Muntakim	The Avenger
81.	Al-'Afuw	The Pardoner
82.	Ar-Ra'uf	The Kind
83.	Malik ul-Mulk	The Ruler of the Kingdom
84.	Dhu'l-Jalah wa'l-Ikram	The Lord of Majesty and Liberality
85.	Al-Muksit	The Equitable
86.	Al-Jami'	The Collector
87.	Al-Ghani	The Independent
88.	Al-Mughni	The Enricher
89.	Al-Mu'ti	The Giver
90.	Al-Mani'	The Withholder
91.	Az-Zarr	The Distresser
92.	An-Nafi'	The Profiter
93.	An-Nur	The Light
94.	Al-Hadi	The Guide
95.	Al-Badi'	The Incomparable
96.	Al-Baki	The Enduring
97.	Al-Warith	The Heir
98.	Ar-Rashid	The Director
99.	As-Sabur	The Patient

various diseases, and their names can be used talismanically. Table 6.3 on pages 80–81 presents a list of Saints who are generally regarded as patrons and protectors in this way. The accompanying Table 6.4 on page 82 shows which Saints to invoke for specific purposes.

By no means all inscriptive talismans are made up of names. Many are composed of connected linguistic statements, and the thinking behind these differs to some extent from other aspects of talismanic thought.

The first important distinction is between pictographic writing—such as the Egyptian hieroglyphs and the Chinese ideograms—which does not in itself provide any clue to spoken language, and writing which clearly indicates pronunciation. The actual speaking aloud of a name or of words has always been regarded as potentially magical. The saying of a word aloud involves the use of the breath, which was regarded by older civilizations, and is still regarded by many so-called primitive societies, as the life force, as the spirit (*spiritus* meaning breath) of the human individual. The saying of a name gave the speaker power over the person, force, or object which bore that name, for the saying of the name brought the bearer of it distinctly to mind, and therefore actually into one's presence. Of course, the name had to be pronounced with a special kind of concentration and in a special tone of voice, otherwise all conversation could become hazardous and all expressions of disagreement dangerous. From this beginning arose the stylized speech of magical statements and incantatory formulae and, ultimately, poetry. The importance of names was such that in some societies people kept one of their names secret so that nobody could pronounce it and thus gain power over them. This notion of the secret name has remained a part of magical tradition, in that members of occult societies always have names whose significance is clear only to members of the society. Many magical books—indeed most of them—have been published under pseudonyms partly because of this tradition.

Just as the saying of the name had to be in a special voice, so the writing of it for magical purposes had to be made quite different

Table 6.2. The Ten Names of God (Kabbalistic)

1. Eheia	The Essence of Divinity
2. Jod	Wisdom
3. Elohim	Providence and Understanding
4. El	Mercy, Grace, Piety, Magnificence
5. Elohim Gibor	Judgment and Power
6. Eloha	Glory and Beauty
7. Adonai Sabaoth	Justice, Triumph, Victory, Eternity
8. Elohim Sabaoth	Agreement and Piety
9. Sadai	Omnipotence
10. Adonai Melech	Empire

Table 6.3 Patron Saints

Of Bell Founders	Saint Agatha (Emblem: Two breasts on a dish)
Of Boy Scouts	Saint George (Emblem: A red cross on a white ground)
Of Children	Saint Nicholas (Emblem: Three Balls)
Of Circus Folk	Saint Julian the Hospitaller
Of Cripples	Saint Giles
Of Domestic Servants	Saint Zita (Emblem: A bunch of keys)
Of Drunkards	Saint Ambrose
Of Emigrants	Saint Frances Cabrini
Of Farriers	Saint Eligius (or Eloi)
Of Ferrymen	Saint Julian the Hospitaller
Of Foreign Missionaries	Saint Francis Xavier
Of Gardeners	Saint Fiachra (Emblem: A Spade)
Of Gunners	Saint Barbara (Emblem: A Tower)
Of Hunters	Saint Hubert (Emblem: A Stag or Hind)
Of Innkeepers	Saint Julian the Hospitaller
Of the Insane	Saint Dympna of Gheel
Of Journalists	Saint Francis de Sales
Of Leatherworkers	Saints Crispin and Crispinian (Emblem: A Last)
Of Lovers	Saint Valentine
Of Medical Doctors	Saint Pantaleon
Of Merchants	Saint Nicholas (Emblem Three Balls)
Of Metal Workers	Saint Eligius (or Eloi)
Of Midwives	Saint Peter Nolesco
Of Miners	Saint Barbara (Emblem: A Tower)
Of Musicians	Saint Cecilia (Emblem: An Organ)
Of Nurses	Saint Camillus de Lellis, Saint John of God
Of Pawnbrokers	Saint Nicholas (Emblem: Three Balls)

Table 6.3 Patron Saints (continued)

Of the Poor	Saint Giles
Of Prisoners	Saint Leonard the Hermit
Of Sailors.....................	Saint Erasmus (or Elmo) (Emblem: A Windlass)
Of Shoemakers	Saints Crispin and Crispinian (Emblem: A Last)
Of the Sick:..................	Saint Michael the Archangel
Of Smiths	Saint Eligius (or Eloi)
Of Soldiers	Saint George (Emblem: A Red Cross on a white ground), and Saint Nicholas (Emblem: Three Balls)
Of Students of the Natural Sciences	Saint Albert the Great
Of Trappers	Saint Hubert (Emblem: A Stag or Hind)
Of Travellers	Saint Christopher
Of Workers for Internaional Justice and Harmony	Saint Martin de Porres

from normal writing, simply to establish that the words were being used magically. Hence, names or words are reproduced using materials not usually used for day to day communication, and sometimes upon extremely valuable materials, such as gemstones, gold, and silver. The medium used may also differ from the norm—the most obvious instance of this is the use of blood as ink; this clearly establishes the intent of the words, for blood is as much a vital power as breath. Some talismanic writing has used other fluids, and special inks have been constructed for magical use.

There are a number of specially contrived magical alphabets in existence, and these not only establish that the writing is magical, but also make it unintelligible to all but initiates. The most famous of these is the Enochian alphabet (see Table 6.5 on page 83) which was brought to light by Dr. John Dee, the astrologer of Queen Elizabeth I. This alphabet forms part of an Enochian Language obtained through the clairvoyant skills of Dee's colleague Edward Kelley. In structure the alphabet is not unlike Hebrew, for the majority of the vowel sounds have no letters and must be supplied

Table 6.4 Saints to Invoke

When in Desperate Difficulty.	Saint Jude
Against Disasters at Sea	Saint Sinach Ma Dara
Against Disease in men and animals	Saint Blaise (Emblem: A Comb or Two Crossed Candles)
In Emergencies	Saint Expeditus
Against Epilepsy	Saint Dympna of Gheel and Saint Vitus (Emblem: A Dog or a Rooster)
Against Eye Disease.........	Saint Lucy (Emblem: Two eyes in a dish)
Against Fire..................	Saint Agatha (Emblem: Two breasts on a dish)
Against Haemerroids	Saint Fiachra (Emblem: A Spade)
Against Headaches	Saint Aedh
Against Insanity.............	Saint Dympna of Gheel
Against Lightning	Saint Barbara (Emblem: A Tower)
To Discover Lost Objects	Saint Antony (Emblem: A Bell and a Pig)
Against all Physical Disease......................	Saint Rock (Emblem: A Dog)
Against Syphilis.............	Saint Fiachra (A Spade)
Against Toothache	Saint Appolonia (Emblem: Forceps gripping a tooth)

by the reader or speaker. Another famous alphabet is that attributed to "Honorius the Theban" (see Figure 6.1 on page 84); it may originate as late as the seventeenth century or as early as the thirteenth; there is no telling. Similarly constructed is the Alphabet of the Magi (see Figure 6.2 on page 85), first presented to the general public by Paul Christian in his *Histoire de la Magie* (1870). The three Angelic alphabets (see Figure 6.3 on pages 86-87) presented by Ambelain in his *La Kabbale Pratique* are composed of little more than reworked Hebrew letters. Nevertheless, all these alphabets served

Table 6.5 The Enochian Alphabet

Enochian Alphabet	Symbol Title	English Equivalent	Enochian Alphabet	Symbol Title	English Equivalent
	Pe	B		Mals	P
	Veh	C or K		Ger	Q
	Ged	G		Drun	N
	Gal	D		Pal	X
	Orth	F		Med	O
	Un	A		Don	R
	Graph	E		Ceph	Z
	Tal	M		Vau	U, V, W
	Gon	I, Y, J		Fam	S
	Na-hath	H		Gisa	T
	Ur	L			

their purpose to keep one mode of writing pure of all mundane connections, therefore make it effective for magical purposes. Numbers also occur in talismans and very few secret ways of presenting numbers are to be found. Perhaps the only one that is at all well known is that provided by Francis Barrett in *The Magus* (1801) which is reproduced in Figure 6.4 on page 88.

Magical alphabets are often used by makers of esoteric talismans, and the letters usually spell out names of power. Talismans of this kind differ very little from those esoteric talismans discussed elsewhere in this book, save in their almost total reliance upon the "spoken" word. Other talismans, however, are composed not of names only but of coherent sentences and of passages from holy books.

The use of passages from holy books as talismans extends as far back as writing itself, and indeed probably began as soon as traditional wisdom became available in written form. There are many talismans which combine both pictographic and written elements. Some of the most interesting are the cylinder seals of Babylon, Assyria, and Egypt. The cylinder seal was, as its name suggests, a cylindrical object frequently made of precious stone, the magical significances of which I have discussed in Chapter 5. These seals were used to seal contracts. They were rolled onto a wet clay

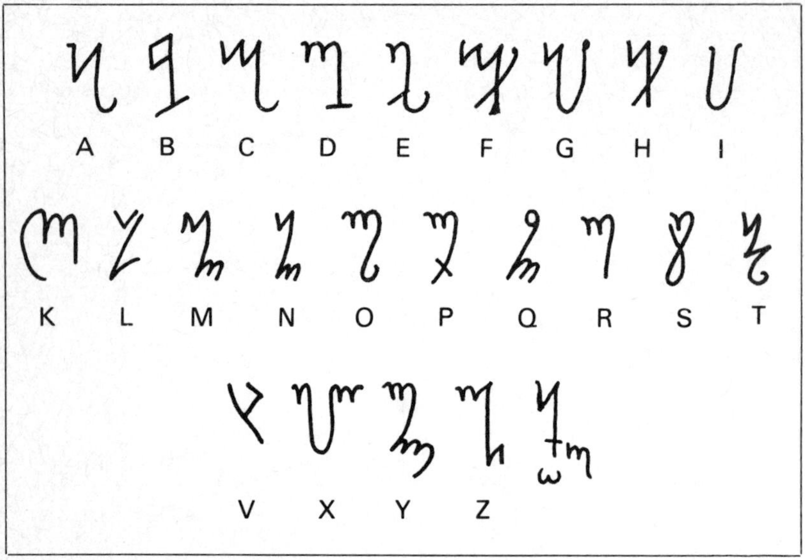

Figure 6.1 Alphabet of Honorius the Theban. Note there is no "j" or "u" in this alphabet. The "w" symbol following the "z" has no equivalent in the Roman alphabet.

tablet and left an impression which clearly identified the owner of the seal. Frequently, the name was often accompanied by a hieroglyph or inscribed picture of a god, and this meant that anyone who broke the agreement thus sealed, or who disobeyed the orders made in the document, was defying the god. Cylinder seals bearing the names of gods were also used as protective talismans and worn around the neck. In Egypt, these talismans were commonly made of bone, ivory, bronze, copper, stone, or blue porcelain. The image or hieroglyph of the god was often accompanied by an invocatory prayer to that god—several of this kind of talisman portray the Sun god.

The Hebrews appear to have been among the first to use talismans that are entirely written. On their foreheads they wore frontlet bands made of skins which were inscribed with religious text, such as: "Hear, O Israel: The Lord our God is one Lord; and thou shall love the Lord thy God with all thine heart, and with all

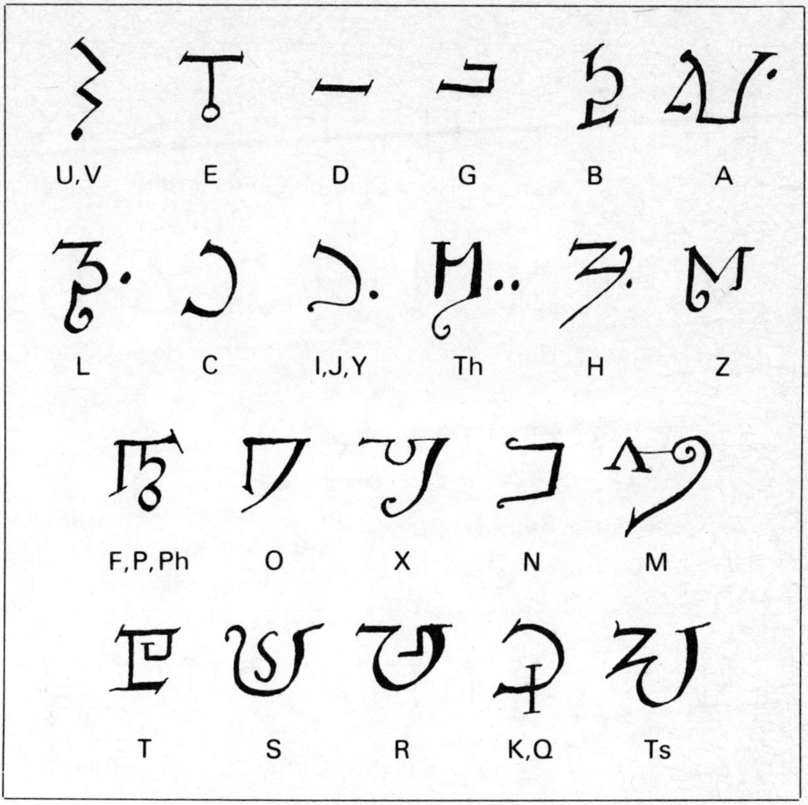

Figure 6.2 Alphabet of the Magi.

thy soul, and with all thy might." *(Deuteronomy, 6:4-5).* These talismans were called phylacteries, and were worn on the hand and on the left arm as well as the forehead. When the inscribed leather strip was hung on the doorpost of the house, it was a talisman called the Mezuzah.

Many of the inscriptions used in these talismans are clearly intended as protections against ill fortune and the evil eye. One is "Thou shalt not be afraid for the terror by night; not for the arrow that flieth by day; not for the pestilence that walketh in darkness; nor for the destruction that waketh at noonday." The whole of

A

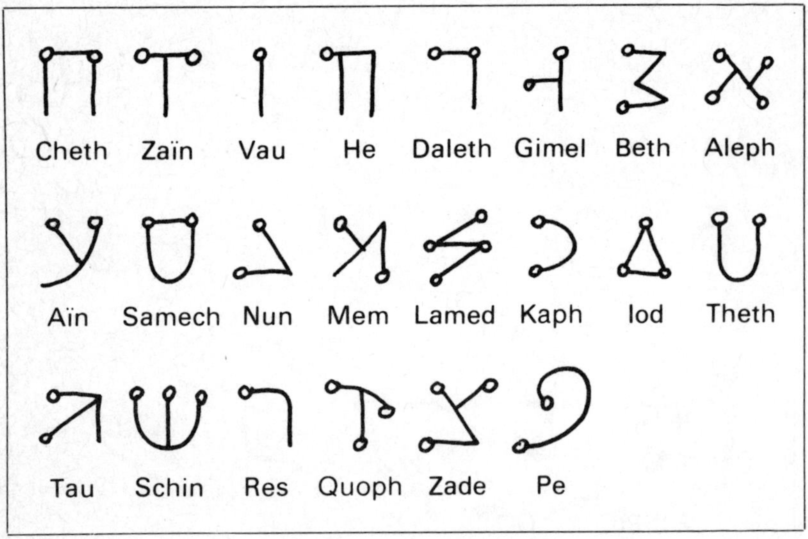
Cheth
Zaïn
Vau
He
Daleth
Gimel
Beth
Aleph
Aïn
Samech
Nun
Mem
Lamed
Kaph
Iod
Theth
Tau
Schin
Res
Quoph
Zade
Pe

B

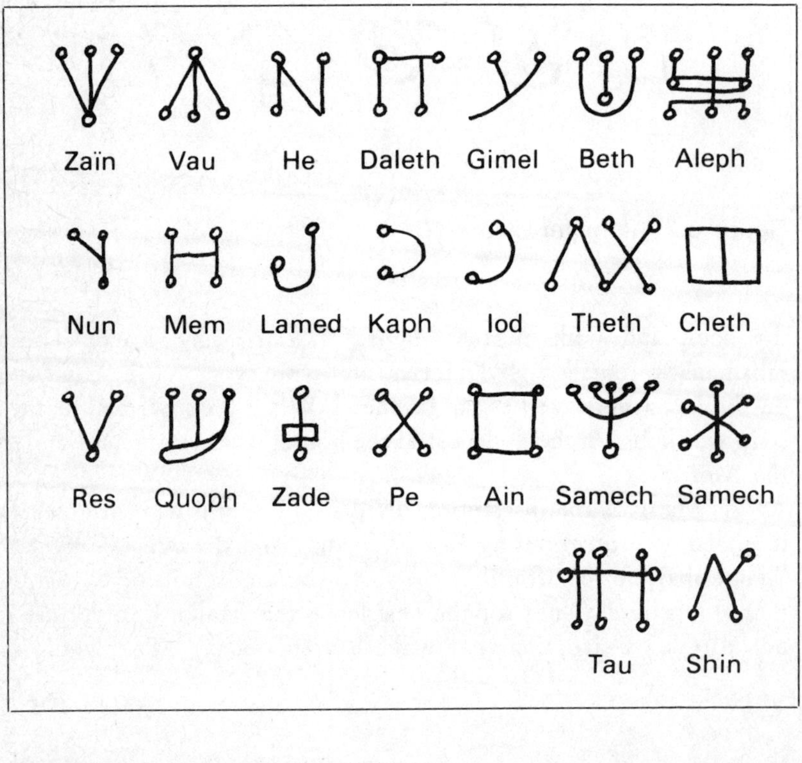
Zaïn
Vau
He
Daleth
Gimel
Beth
Aleph
Nun
Mem
Lamed
Kaph
Iod
Theth
Cheth
Res
Quoph
Zade
Pe
Ain
Samech
Samech
Tau
Shin

C

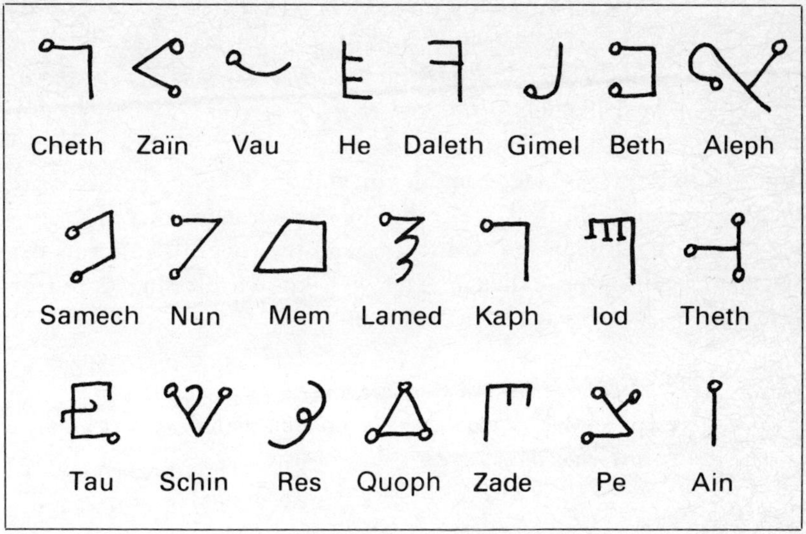

Figure 6.3 The Three Angelic Alphabets: a) The Celestial alphabet (an angelic script); b) the Malachim alphabet (an angelic script); c) the alphabet called "du passage du fleuve," or "passing the river."

Psalm 97 was written on leather and arranged in the form of a seven branched candlestick. This psalm reads:

> 1 *O praise the LORD, all ye nations: praise him all ye people.*
> 2 *For his merciful kindness is great towards us: and the truth of the LORD endureth for ever.*

Another favorite psalm used for talismans was *Psalm 121:*

> 1 *I will lift up mine eyes unto the hills, from whence cometh my help.*
> 2 *My help cometh from the LORD, which made heaven and earth.*
> 3 *He will not suffer thy foot to be moved: he that keepeth thee will not slumber.*
> 4 *Behold, he that keepeth Israel will neither slumber nor sleep.*
> 5 *The LORD is thy keeper; the LORD is thy shade upon thy right hand.*

6 *The sun shall not smite thee by day, nor the moon by night.*
7 *The LORD shall preserve thee from all evil: he shall preserve thy soul.*
8 *The LORD shall preserve thy going out, and thy coming in, from this time forth, and even for evermore.*

Some talismans included double meanings. One uses the word "ayin," meaning both a well and an eye, in a text from *Genesis* which reads: "Joseph is a fruitful bough by a well," and thus is a talisman against the evil eye. The well-known blessing of Aaron *(Numbers 6: 24-26)* was also a favorite:

> *The Lord bless thee, and keep thee; the Lord make his face shine upon thee and be gracious unto thee; the Lord lift up his countenance upon thee, and give thee peace.*

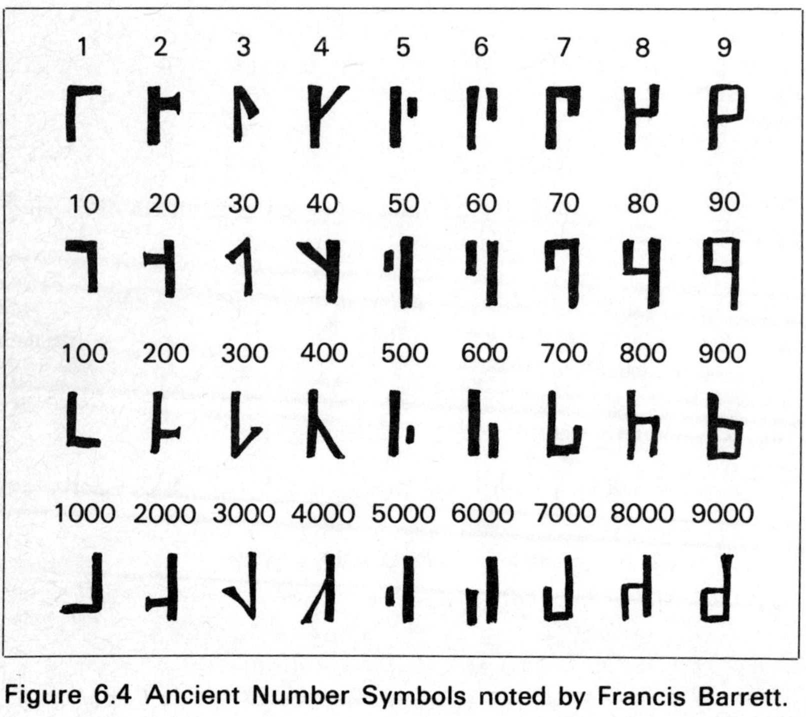

Figure 6.4 Ancient Number Symbols noted by Francis Barrett.

Mohammedans used, and still use, the text of the *Koran* in the same way as the Jews use the text of their holy books. They regard the whole of the *Koran* as a talisman and even in the first years of the twentieth century few people from the Mohammedan countries would travel without a copy. After photolithography came into use, copies of the whole of the *Koran* were made measuring no more than 1 inch by ¾ inch by 7/16 inch, and enclosed in carrying cases made of metal with a ring attached to them so that they could be worn round the travelers' necks. These are also equipped with a magnifying glass so that they can be read. Some chapters and passages of the *Koran* are written on parchment or, recently, paper, and carried in specially made containers. Some are carved on precious or semi-precious stones.

The texts used are selected both to assert the general power and benevolence of the one true god, and to defend the talisman wearer from demons and from the evil eye. *Surah* (Chapter) *112* is often used:

> *1 Say: He, Allah is One.*
> *2 Allah the self subsisting.*
> *3 He begetteth not, and He was not begotten.*
> *4 And there is no one like unto Him.*

Surah 2, v 256 may remind us in part of *Psalm 121:*

> *God: There is no GOD but He; the living the self subsisting;*
>
> *Neither slumber nor sleep seizeth Him;*
>
> *To Him belongeth whatsoever is in heaven, and on earth,*
>
> *Who is he that can intercede with Him but through His good pleasure?*
>
> *He knoweth that which is past, and that which is to come unto them;*
>
> *And they shall not comprehend anything of His knowledge, but so far as He pleaseth.*
>
> *His throne is extended over heaven and earth, and the preservation of both is no burden unto Him.*
>
> *He is the High, the Mighty.*

The opening prayer of the *Koran,* the *Fatihat,* is also popular:

In the name of Allah, the Merciful, the Compassionate,
1 *Praise be unto Allah, the Lord of the worlds.*
2 *The Merciful, the Compassionate.*
3 *King of the Day of Judgement.*
4 *Thee do we worship, of Thee we entrust for help.*
5 *Direct us in the path which is straight.*
6 *The path of those on whom Thou hast shown favour.*
7 *Not of those with whom Thou art angry. Nor those who wander.*

From *Surah 113* the following text is used to avert evil:

In the Name of God, the Merciful, the Compassionate.
1 *Say: I fly for refuge to the Lord of the Daybreak.*
2 *From the evil things which He hath created.*
3 *And from the evil of the night when it hath come.*
4 *And from the evil of women who are blowers on knots.*
5 *And from the evil of the envious man when he hath envied.*

The phrase "blowers on knots" refers to the practice of tying knots in string while reciting spells intended to do harm to others; the knots are intended to keep the evil spell secure and unbreakable, at least until they were untied. During the making of these spells, the spell maker would blow on the knots as they were being tied.

While all these passages of holy books are used as talismans proper, they are also clearly used as prayers—the prayer is being repeated all the time the talisman is worn. In some instances it can actually be read by the wearer; in others, of course, it it written or inscribed in so small a script or arranged in so complex a pattern that this is not possible.

Many societies have used passages from scripture in this way. The Buddhist monks of the Temple of the Tooth in Kandy, Ceylon, inscribe passages on dried *bo* leaves for talismans to be given to visitors and worshippers. Tibetan models of the Buddha made of cast metal usually have a cavity in their base which often contains written material as well as, or instead of, relics and sometimes precious stones. The Chinese have always used talismans of the written, or rather painted, kind. Indeed this kind of talisman is common in all literate societies.

It is as common today, moreover, as it has been. The small discs and badges inscribed with the ten commandments which were fashionable in the nineteenth century can still be found, and are still being made.

Many talismanic tattoos consist of passages from the Bible. Some of the most popular are "Jesus saves," and "The Lord is my Shepherd, I shall not want," and "God is my strength." Many of these are accompanied by religious pictures, which range from portraits of the Madonna and Child, and Christ on the Cross, to the whole of the Last Supper. Sometimes the whole of the Lord's Prayer is used as a tattoo. This, like other written talismans we have been surveying, might be called not simply a verbal but a discursive talisman.

Not all verbal talismans are discursive in this fashion, of course. Some are simply arrangements of words, or letters. One such is the Agla, which was used by Sir John Dee and was popular in the Middle Ages as a talisman against fever. The letters A G L A stand for Ate Gebir Leilam Adonai ("Thou art mighty for ever, O Lord") and these four letters were inscribed in the four quarters of a mandala on a brooch or ring.

There is a Hebrew amulet which consists of the five letters of the name Elohim, one of the names of God, arranged in a square of 25 letters. Sometimes texts are manipulated in this fashion also. The most widely known letters square is the SATOR talisman in which the letters spell out the same words both vertically and horizontally, whether read upwards or downwards or from the right or the left:

S	A	T	O	R
A	R	E	P	O
T	E	N	E	T
O	P	E	R	A
R	O	T	A	S

The Latin sentence thus spelt out can be translated as "Arepo, the sower, holds back the works that are being done with his wheels" or, more simply, "Arepo , the sower, holds back the work with his wheels." Arepo is not a known name. It could, possibly, be a near anagram for Ore'a, an angel guard of the fourth hall of heaven, recorded in Hebrew lore. This does not seem likely. Arel, one of the angels of fire, would be more appropriate as this talisman is most commonly reported as being an implement to put out a fire. If the letters are written on a wooden plate and the plate is thrown into the fire, the fire will go out. This was so firmly believed that in Saxony, in 1742, people were ordered to have these plates to hand for fighting fires. If written in pigeon's blood on parchment and held in the left hand, the SATOR talisman will grant your wishes, according to one old manuscript. If it is hung around the neck of an animal or a human being before dawn on a Friday at an hour which has an uneven number, and if it is augmented by writing beneath it the following, then it will drive away the plague and foul air.

+ J + C + S + H S b y l S a n n e t
U S M m a t e r o n n y + S b a b e 2
S +

It may also be used to discover a witch if it is hung as before but augmented with the inscription + I N + R I + at the top and C + M + B + at the bottom. To make this work, the afflicted person should also be given a mixture of three pinches of flour and three of salt and three pinches of dust created from the timber of the house by filing the wood. The witch will then appear. If you simply wish to protect yourself or your animals from witchcraft and the evil eye, it is sufficient to hang the basic square around the neck of the one requiring protection.

This may also be hung around the neck of a cow after it has calved, or when it has the fever. It should be hung around the neck of the animal on a Friday between twelve noon and one o'clock. This will drive away fever and ensure a good milk yield. If it is put into a leather bag together with roots of the St. John's Wort and another unidentified herb called *moto* and hung around your neck, witches will not be able to bear your company. In this case, the first three lines should be followed with additional words. The first line should be augmented with " + Cross of Christ mildepos," the second with " + Cross of Christ mesepos," and the third with "+ Cross of Christ Habenepos."

In all instances, this talisman is used to stop a destructive process. It may be that the correct way to read the Latin is not as one complete sentence, but as a sentence accompanied by a magical verbal gesture. Thus: SATOR (Arepo) TENET (Opera) ROTAS. The sentence now reads: "The Sower holds back the wheels," and the two words in brackets are simply an indication of what the Sower is doing—altering the backward movement of events, of the Opera, the works, that which is being done, to the forward movement. It might also be noted that if the word Opera is written around a wheel, the counterclockwise movement of the wheel would bring the word Arepo. One might therefore like to translate the remaining words, SATOR TENET ROTAS freely as The Sower (or Creator), holds (or controls, retains mastery of), the wheels (the Wheels of Life). Another interpretation is based upon the notion that the talisman is a Christian one, for it has been found inscribed in a number of bibles of the period 700-800 A.D. This suggests that

SATOR AREPO TENET OPERA ROTAS

is an anagram of PATER NOSTER twice repeated, together with the letters O and A standing for Alpha and Omega, the beginning and the end, which placed together in this fashion are a symbol of Christ. Unfortunately, for this view there is only one N is the sentence. On the other hand it can be maintained that as the letter N occurs at the very center of the square, it can be regarded as having double value. A less well known anagrammatic solution is that which suggests it is an anagram of PATER NOSTER (Our Father) SOTER (Savior) PATERA (Offering Dish), which has the virtue of being a version of the God the Father, God the Son, and the Virgin Mary who was often referred to as a holy vessel. Latinists may like to attempt further solutions.

There are other equally mysterious verbal talismans made along the same lines as this one. The most well known are those of the magician Abremalin; the manuscript containing them was written in the eighteenth century, but dated 1458, and was claimed to be translated from the Hebrew. One of these is very close to the SATOR talisman, and because the similarity lies in the inclusion of the two words AREPO and OPERA, it tends to support the view that these two words are not to be considered as part of the statement, but rather as an indication that "works" are being done. The square goes:

S	A	L	O	M
A	R	E	P	O
L	E	M	E	L
O	P	E	R	A
M	O	L	A	S

If we extract the three words which carry meaning we get SALOM LEMEL MOLAS. If we are to believe that this was originally in Hebrew we can ignore the vowels, for written Hebrew does not have letters for vowel sounds. We must, however, because of the word OPERA assume that the words were originally Latin, even though written in Hebrew form. If we perform this feat of mental juggling we get SLM LML MLS, which could be read in the kind of Latin frequent in these maneuvers as SEMEL (At a word) LIMULA (squinting) MULSA (Sweet as honey). This is probably as good an interpretation as any, for the talisman is one to gain the love of a woman. If laid to her bare skin, however briefly, she will fall in love with the man concerned.

Another of Abremalin's talismans is to enable the wearer to fly like a crow. The word ROLOR is supposed to be derived from a Hebrew word ROL which means to move quickly. The other words remain doubtful:

R	O	L	O	R
O	B	U	F	O
L	U	A	U	L
O	F	U	B	O
R	O	L	O	R

This square is interesting in that two of the words are palinodes, and not just the third one, which is always necessary. Another, rather unlikely talismanic square of Abremalin is:

M	I	L	O	N
I	R	A	G	O
L	A	M	A	L
O	G	A	R	I
N	O	L	I	M

If this is written on parchment and placed on the top of your head, you will be given insight into the past, present and future. Whether or not you will be given insight as to the meaning of the words on the talisman is not clear.

The other squares of Abremalin are just as difficult to interpret as the ones we have seen, and perhaps we have looked at enough of them. There are, however, other verbal talismans which are possibly even more baffling. One consists of a stick upon which the following letters have been cut or written:

+ Z + D I A + B + Z + S A

B Z + H V W F + B E R S + + +

If this stick is laid upon a valuable object no thief will be able to steal it.

Another talisman of this kind is one against the plague. If the following is written on a new piece of parchment and buried under the house it will prevent the plague arriving:

Z + O A + B I Z + S A B + Z H G F + B F R S +

A talisman against sudden shooting pains consists of the following written upon paper:

ARILL. AT. GOLL. GOTTZO.

If you wish to improve your marksmanship place the following inscription under your gun barrel:

D E W D W S H H D F S K O M W V R

V J S K N U F M U E S O Mi

When a women is suffering labor pains you can alleviate them by writing on a piece of paper:

A b h z P O b L 9 h b m g n Subratum nome nex gr.

[The Woman's Name]

+ Ecgitar + Circabato + Bessiabato + Argon + Vigaro Tanet.

This should then be placed in a bag of leather which must be sewn up with the seam on the right hand side without there being any knots or loose threads and hung on the patient during an hour with an uneven number.

If you wish to make yourself invulnerable to gun shot, carry the following words about with you:

Light, Beff, Cletemati, Adonai, Cleona, Florit.

Or the following:

LIGHT, BETTER, CLOTENTAL,

SOBATH, ADONAY, ALBOA, FLORAT.

To cure or prevent cataract, hang the following verbal talisman around the neck:

GAA, SAGA, FASSAA

I have not attempted to explain these verbal talismans because I cannot do so. It seems clear that all these letters were originally symbols for specific spiritual forces, and that we have now lost the key to them. To judge from the alternative talismans against gunshot it also seems that the texts are probably garbled. It is doubtful if talismans of this kind can have any effect for those who are unable to imbue them with energy because they do not understand the forces to which they refer. It is likely that in the Middle Ages they had considerable meaning, and the letters were most carefully chosen.

Another less cryptic but possibly more ingenious form of written talisman is formed on the basis of the dwindling spell. This is a verbal spell in which a disorder is told to dwindle away by reciting an ever diminishing series of words, sounds or numbers. One might begin by saying that there were nine spirits, and then eight, and then seven, dwindling down to zero. Many of these dwindling spells were written out on paper and bound to the patient's body. It is not always easy to be sure whether talismans of this kind were read aloud or simply worn. The Hebrew talisman against both eye disease and the evil eye is written out in the form of a triangle with the point downwards; this, if pronounced aloud, would read Shebriri, Briri, Riri, Iri, Ri, I, and then, of course, silence. This is a true talisman, however, in that it is worn on all occasions and not simply read aloud when needed.

The most famous of all the talismans utilizing dwindling spells is, of course, the Abracadabra. This word, now used as a general word of power by illusionists when taking rabbits out of top hats or performing other feats of legerdemain has baffled almost everyone who has attempted to find a meaning for it. Perhaps the most sensible solution to the problem was offered by Bischoff,[2] who suggested that ABRACADABRA is a corruption, probably caused by oral repetition of the Chaldee words ABBADA KE DABRA which he translates as "Perish like the word." This command was directed specifically at the fever. The ABRACADABRA talisman is usually written out in this fashion:

ABRACADABRA
ABRACADABR
ABRACADAB
ABRACADA
ABRACAD
ABRACA
ABRAC
ABRA
ABR
AB
A

[2]Dr. Erich Bischoff, *The Kabbalah: An Introduction to Jewish Mysticism and Secret Doctrine.* Originally published in Germany. English translation published by Samuel Weiser, Inc., York Beach, ME, 1985.

The same dwindling formula is used on a Hebrew talisman against fire. This consists of a hexagram on the six sides of which are written the names of God, and the spell itself written on the front and back of the parchment consists of the Hebrew for "And it (meaning the fire) dwindled," this being from the second verse of the 11th chapter of *Numbers,* which reads:

> And the people cried unto Moses; and when Moses prayed unto the Lord the fire was quenched.

No talisman of this or any other kind can be expected to be effective if it has not been made with the right kind of concentration, or in some way blessed and imbued with energy. In *Amulets and Talismans*, Sir E.A. Wallis Budge gives the text of a talisman together with the rules for making it—this may be accepted as a typical example of the method generally used in consecrating talismans of the kind we have been describing. The talismanic words are:

> Ab Abr Abra Abrak Abraka
> Abrakal Abrakala Abrakal
> Abraka Abrak Abra Abr Ab.

> "And the people called unto Moses and Moses prayed to God, and the fire abated" (Numbers 6:2.). "May healing come from heaven from all kinds of fever and consumption-heat to N son of N. Amen. Amen. Amen. Selah. Selah. Selah." Here is the perfect Hebrew amulet which contains (1) The magical NAME Abrakala; (2) The TEXT from the Bible; (3) The PRAYER, which is the equivalent of the pagan incantation; (4) The THREEFOLD AMEN and the THREEFOLD SELAH. Dr. Gaster (Hastings' *Encyc.*, vol. iii. p. 455) has translated the directions for writing this amulet. The Name must be written exactly as it is written in the scroll of the Law on specially prepared parchment. It must be written with square or "Ashuri" letters so that no letter shall touch the next, i.e. there must be a free margin round each letter. It must be written in purity and whilst fasting. It must be wrapped in leather or in some soft rag,

and be wrapped round with a piece of clean leather. It is to be hung on the neck of the patient without his knowing it or when he is asleep, and he is not to look at it for the next twenty-four hours. The lines for the writing must be drawn on the hairy side of the parchment and the writing is to be done on the flesh side, and in the name of the patient. The parchment must be cut and the lines drawn on it in the patient's name. When the writer dips his pen into properly prepared ink he must say: "In the Name of Shaddai who created heaven and earth. I, N, the son of N, write this *Kemi'a* for X, son of X, to heal him of every kind of fever." And then he must say the blessing of the *Kemi'a* as follows: "Blessed art Thou, O Lord our God, Who hast sanctified Thy great Name and has revealed it to Thy pious ones, to show its great power and might in the language [in which it is expressed] in the writing of it, and in the utterance of the mouth. Blessed art Thou O Lord, holy King, whose great Name be exalted."[3]

When we study inscribed talismans, we see how many talismans have been made in terms of a complex system of ideas. In this Chapter, we have seen them related to both Mohammedan and Jewish religious beliefs and other views. One of the oldest of systems is that presented by astrology. We will look at astrological talismans in the next chapter.

---

[3]Sir E. A. Wallis Budge, *Amulets and Superstitions*, 1930. Reissued as *Amulets and Talismans*, University Books, New York, 1968, pp. 221-222.

Chapter 7

Astrological Talismans

It is the stars,
The stars above us, govern our conditions.

Shakespeare
King Lear, Iv.iii, 34.

Modern astrology does not pay much attention to talismans. Most of the current works in the field mention them extremely briefly, if at all. Nevertheless, astrology does establish correspondences between bodily weaknesses and astral influences, and it is clear that effective talismans can be made along lines proved by modern astrologers.

Signs of the Zodiac

Let's examine the qualities and symbols associated with the twelve signs of the zodiac.

Aries (♈) rules the head and Arians are consequently subject to headaches. Because Aries is opposite to Libra in the Zodiac, and Libra rules the kidneys, the headaches may be associated with kidney disorders. Arians are adventurous, energetic, and freedom loving, but inclined to be egotistical, impatient, and pugnacious. The Arian color is fiery red, the metal copper, the stone the ruby or the diamond. Among the plants it is associated with the tiger lily, the honeysuckle, the geranium and the thistle, and among the trees it is associated with blackberries, hawthorn, and anything that bears thorns. Its symbols are the owl and the ram.

Taurus (♉) rules the neck and throat, and Taureans are prone to catch cold easily and to suffer from laryngitis. As it is opposite to Scorpio which rules the sexual organs it is possible that sexual difficulties may result in psychosomatic illnesses of the throat. Taureans are reliable, patient, strong-minded, persevering and warm-hearted, but inclined also to be stubborn, self-indulgent and conservative. The Taurean colors are pale blue, pink and dark green; the metal is copper; the stone is sapphire or topaz. It is associated with the rose, the poppy, the violet and the foxglove, and, among trees, with the ash, the apple and the cypress. Its symbol is the bull.

Gemini (♊) rules the ears, arms, hands, lungs, and shoulders and Geminis are therefore likely to break arms and collarbones, and to suffer from bronchitis. As this sign is opposite Sagittarius, which rules the hips and thighs and the liver, Geminis may suffer in these areas also. Geminis are lively, versatile, intelligent and often garrulous, but sometimes cunning, over-inquisitive, hypocritical, and inclined to nervous tension. Some say the Gemini color is chestnut brown, others that it is bright yellow, but all colors are relevant; the metal is mercury; the stone is agate or tourmaline. Gemini is associated with lavender, lily of the valley, and orchids and with all nut bearing trees. Its symbol is the magpie.

Leo (♌) rules the heart and the spine, and Leo types are prone to heart attacks, which may be caused by defects in the circulation and by hardening arteries, as this sign is opposite to Aquarius which rules the circulation of the blood. Leo characters are generous, creative, enthusiastic, sometimes histrionic, but can become conceited, pompous, and overbearing. Leo's colors are gold, orange and golden yellow; the metal is gold; the stone is ruby or cat's eye. Leo is associated with marigolds and sunflowers, and with orange trees, lemon trees and the bay and the palm. Its symbol is the lion.

Cancer (♋) rules the stomach, the intestines and women's breasts, and Cancerians tend to suffer from nervous dyspepsia, and from stomach ulcers. These may in part be caused by mouth and dental infections as the ruler of the mouth and teeth and of bones generally is Capricorn, which is placed opposite to Cancer in the Zodiac. The Cancerian is imaginative, sensitive, sympathetic and often shrewd, but can suffer from moodiness, quickness of temper and hypersensitivity which may lead to self-pity and emotional instability. The Cancerian colors are silver and the more subtle tones of green and gray; the metal is silver; the precious stone is the pearl or amber. The plants associated with Cancer are the lotus, all wildflowering plants, and trees particularly rich in sap such as gum trees, and pines. Its symbols are both the crab and the turtle.

Virgo (♍) rules the intestines and the nervous system, and, like Cancerians, Virgos are subject to indigestion and ulcers caused by nervous tension and stress. Virgos are modest, precise in thought, and tidy, but tend to be hypercritical, over-conventional, and fussy and tend to become neurotically anxious over details. The Virgo colors are dark blues, greys and browns; the metal is mercury; the stones are sardonyx and peridot. Virgo is associated with snowdrops, lilies, and all small bright flowers, and nut bearing trees. Its symbol is the Virgin.

Libra (♎) rules the kidneys, and Librans tend to suffer from kidney trouble which may be associated with nervous tensions caused by the adrenal glands ruled by Aries. The Libran is easy going, romantically inclined, idealistic and fair minded, but can be indecisive and too easily influenced by the views of others. The Libran colors are pink, pale blue and watery green; the metal is copper; the stone is sapphire or emerald. Libra is associated with all blue flowers, with the larger varieties of rose, and with the ash tree. Its symbols are the scales and the elephant.

Scorpio (♏) rules the genitals and Scorpios suffer from being highly sexed, and are therefore prone to nervous frustration and emotional difficulties, which sometimes cause throat troubles as their opposite number is Taurus. Scorpios are very emotional and imaginative, as well as persevering and subtle, but can also be sly, stubborn, and jealous. The Scorpio color is vermilion or dark red; the metal is iron; the stone opal or ammonite. Scorpio is associated with all dark red flowers, and with blackthorn and cactus. Its symbols are the wolf, lobster, beetle, as well as the scorpion.

Sagittarius (♐) rules the thighs, hips and liver, and Sagittarians have a tendency to overweight. They are optimistic, adaptable, jovial, candid, and sincere with a good fund of commonsense, but can be tactless, boisterous, and inclined to exaggeration. Sagittarian colors are purple, dark blue and sky blue; the metal is tin; the stone is topaz or jacinth. Sagittarius is associated with tomato, asparagus, rush dandelion, and with the mulberry, the ash, the birch and the oak. Its symbols are the horse, dog and centaur.

Capricorn (♑) rules the bones, the teeth, and the knees and Capricornians are liable to suffer dental ailments and weakness of the knee joints. Capricornians are prudent, determined, ambitious and disciplined, with a good sense of humor, though this cannot always save them from becoming rigid in outlook, pessimistic, and mean. The colors are black and dark grey, brown, and deep green; the metal is lead; the stone turquoise or black diamond. Capricorn is associated with thistles, pansies, onions, ivy, willows, pines, elms, poplars, and with cannabis. Its symbols are the ass and the goat.

Aquarius (♒) rules the circulation of the blood and the ankles, and Aquarians are liable to suffer from hardening of the arteries and varicose veins, which may lead to heart disorders as Aquarius is opposite to Leo in the Zodiac which rules the heart. Aquarians are friendly, loyal, idealistic and intellectually inventive, but their very originality can lead them to become eccentric and rebellious, and inclined to cherish unconventionality for its own sake. The Aquarian color is grey or electric blue; the metal is uranium; the stone is amethyst or glass. Aquarius is associated with orchids, coconuts and with fruit trees. Its symbols are the peacock and the eagle.

Pisces (♓) rules the feet, and Pisceans are unduly affected by foot disorders. Pisceans are emotionally sensitive and intuitive, and extremely kind and sympatheic, but their sensibility can lead them to become indecisive and easily confused. The Piscean color is sea green or sea blue; the metal is tin; the stone is moonstone or pearl. Pisces is associated with water lilies, willow trees, fig trees, and the opium poppy. Its symbols are the dolphin, fish and beetle.

The Planets

Just as the signs of the Zodiac affect the human bodily functions, so do the planets, which also have traditional associations with various metals, colors, and plants.

Mercury (☿) affects the brain, the nervous system, and breathing. Its color is yellow; its metal is, obviously, mercury. Its stones are opal and agate. Associated plants are lilies, narcissi, vervain, palm, and the fir tree. Its creatures are the swallow and the ape.

Venus (♀) affects the kidneys, like Libra which it rules; it also affects the throat and especially the parathyroid glands which control the calcium level in the body and therefore have to do with the health of the bones. Its color is green; its metal is copper; its stones are the turquoise and emerald. Associated plants are the aster, rose, clover, daisy, myrtle, and verbena. Its creatures are the sparrow, dove and swan.

Sun (☉) The Sun, like Leo, affects the heart and the spine, and also the thymus, which lies behind the sternum at the very center of the body, and which is largely responsible for enabling the body to fight off diseases caused by bacteria. Its color is gold, which is also its metal; its stone is crysoleth. Associated plants are the vine, the sunflower, the marigold, and the laurel. Its creatures are the lion and the sparrowhawk.

Jupiter (♃) like Sagittarius, rules the liver, and also the pituitary glands which control the body's rate of growth and its production of hormones. Its color is blue; its metal is tin; its precious stones are amethyst and lapis lazuli. Its creature is the eagle.

Moon (☽) The moon affects many parts of the body including the breasts, and the whole of the digestive system, including the pancreas, the liver, and the bile ducts. Its color is silver, which is also its metal. Its stones are crystal, pearl, and moonstone.

Associated plants are the iris, almond, hazel, mugwort, ranunculus. Its creature is the dog.

Pluto (♇) affects the reproductive system, and the body's capacity to produce cells.

Mars (♂) affects the sex glands in both men and women and also the muscles. Its color is red; its metal is iron; its stone is ruby. Associated plants are the briar, buttercup, verbena and wormwood. Its creatures are the horse, bear, and wolf.

Neptune (♆) orders the nervous system in general, and especially the thalamus which is responsible for the efficiency with which the nerve endings in the body transmit their messages to the brain.

Uranus (♅) affects the circulation and the pineal body, or "third eye," which is situated in the center of the forehead, and whose function appears to be entirely perceptive, but perceptive of stimuli which remain unnoticed by other parts of the body.

Saturn (♄) affects the skin, the teeth, the bones, and the gall bladder as well as the frontal part of the pituitary glands. Its color is black and its metal is lead. Its stones are star sapphire and pearl. Associated plants are the monkshood, cypress and opium poppy.

Table 7.1 Signs of the Zodiac and Angelic Rulership

Sign	Governed by	Angel of
Aries	Malahidiel	March
Taurus	Asmodel	April
Gemini	Ambiel	May
Cancer	Muriel	June
Leo	Verchiel	July
Virgo	Hamaliel	August
Libra	Uriel	September
Scorpio	Barbiel	October
Sagittarius	Advachiel	November
Capricorn	Hanael	December
Aquarius	Cambiel	January
Pisces	Barchiel	February

Table 7.2 Governors of the Seven Planets

Planet	Angel or Governor
Sun	Raphael
Venus	Anael
Mercury	Michael
Moon	Gabriel
Saturn	Zaphiel
Jupiter	Zadkiel
Mars	Camael

The information given here is taken from many sources, and some authorities are inevitably in disagreement. This is especially the case with the associated colors, metals and plants, for astrology has developed over a long period and its theories have consequently changed over the centuries. Nevertheless in talismanic magic it is always the intent which is the most important part of the operation, and does not matter a great deal if some of the symbols one uses are somewhat approximate. I have tried, however, in making my list to take a consensus, and also to exclude associations which, for various reasons, seem to me to be somewhat dubious.

Although we have now listed the main functions and qualities of the signs and planets of the zodiac, we have not arrived at anything like a complete picture of the symbolism attached to them or of the traditional views of their powers—and many authorities will inevitably be in disagreement with the correspondences. Indeed, kabbalists and other occultists and mystics have given names to the powers in the planets, and also signs. Consequently, an absolutely comprehensive "character" of any one planet or sign of the Zodiac could occupy many volumes. Nevertheless, anyone wishing to make an astrological talisman might well decide that he could do so with more conviction if he had a named spirit to associate with it. Table 7.1 provides a list of the angels associated with the signs of the Zodiac, while Table 7.2 presents the angels associated with the planets.The old astrologers and occultists took account of only seven planets; Uranus, Neptune, and Pluto were then unknown.

We can now design a simple talisman making use of all this information in a fairly straightforward fashion. In so doing we are not running counter to the views of occultists who have drawn up elaborate methods of making talismans according to kabbalistic thought; we are using exactly the same principles but in a simpler manner.

Let us assume that we wish to create a talisman to protect us against being susceptible to colds and bronchitis. Those born under Taurus and Gemini are particularly prone to these disorders. Mercury governs respiration. We therefore need a talisman which shows, in simple symbolic terms, Mercury controlling Gemini and Taurus. Because Mercury's metal is itself mercury, of which no talisman can be made, we substitute a metal which looks like it, and the usual substitute is tin, though an alloy of silver, tin and mercury would be the ideal prescription. We can take a circle of tin, however, quite easily from our garbage bag, and even though the alloy used in canning is not tin, it is generally known and therefore responded to, as such. The color of Mercury is yellow; a yellow circle should be painted on a circle cut from tin. In the top half of the circle, the sign of Mercury should be painted also in yellow and then, below it, in a much smaller size to show subjection, the sign for Gemini in yellow also (for yellow is a Gemini color), and the sign for Taurus should be painted in pale blue. On the back of the piece of tin should be written the name of the angel of Mercury, Michael. In order to consecrate the talisman and make it operative we should then hold it in the smoke of a fire made of the leaves and stalks of the plants with which it is associated—narcissi and lilies. If the season of the year makes this difficult, it would be just as sensible to hold it in the smoke of any incense or fire which pleases the nostrils and eases the lungs, since as we do this we must concentrate our minds upon the act of deep clean breathing, upon clarity and purity of air, upon all images which we associate with health in the respiratory system. The talisman should then be put in a silken bag (silk being traditionally regarded as an insulator against a field of energy dissipating itself) and it should be worn around the neck of the person for whom it is intended, and whose name must have been in our minds all the time while making the talisman. It need not be kept in the bag of silk when it is being worn, but at other times it should be wrapped up and protected in this fashion.

This is a very simple talisman to make, and other talismans for physical and psychological disorders can easily be made in the same way. The important thing is for the talisman maker to be able to understand fully why each part of the talisman is made in the fashion it is, and what all the parts of it refer to. If materials prove impossible to find or to afford for a sun talisman, gold foil, or even gold paper will do, for the message is of primary importance and the material simply a vehicle for the message. On the other hand, it must be pointed out that metal retains the energy field better than any other material. Still, there are many talisman makers who consider that a well drawn talisman, lettered and painted with care, will operate with total success even if it is made of cardboard. Indeed, many effective talismans have been made this way.

I have already pointed out the importance of the act of consecration. I must underline it here. The symbols used, even on our simple Mercury talisman for bronchitis, are all symbols of multiple powers. Mercury does not only affect the respiratory system, for example, and Gemini rules more than the chest. Similarly, Michael is an angel associated with much more than the planet Mercury. Mercury itself, of course, is regarded as a planet which can bless financial interests and businesses. The act of consecration, therefore, is the most important, for it defines the task the talisman is to perform. Chapter 9 addresses the whole business of consecration in greater detail.

Those who have studied the making of talismans have also pointed out that the talisman that makes use of a particular planet should be made on the day of the week which is ruled by the planet, and others have gone further and suggested that before any talisman is made a full study of the position of the relevant planet in the heavens should be made. It appears to me, however, that only two considerations are of such importance as to be regarded as essential. Firstly, all talismans should be made during the waxing of the moon, and never during its waning, and secondly, one should pick the right day of the week. The days ruled by the planets are as follows:

Sunday. . . Sun
Monday. . . Moon
Tuesday. . . Mars
Wednesday. . . Mercury
Thursday. . . Jupiter
Friday. . . Venus
Saturday. . . Saturn

This scheme leaves the new planets out in the cold; there are no days of the week for Pluto, Neptune, and Uranus. This problem is easily solved: Talismans calling on the power of these planetary powers should be made on *Sunday*, since the Sun is the symbol of universal and all encompassing power.

Talismans of this kind are easy to make and their symbolism is not particularly complicated. There are, however, other astrological talismans which are much more sophisticated. These are based upon the mystical and philosophical system of the Jewish Kabbalah, upon which most kinds of ceremonial magic in the Western world also depend. Understanding of the Kabbalah, indeed, enables one to make many kinds of talisman, including some which we have not yet discussed.

Chapter 8

Kabbalistic Talismans

> *Now there is a traditional correspondence, which modern experiment has shown to be fairly reliable. There is a certain natural connexion between certain letters, words, numbers, gestures, shapes, perfumes and so on, so that any idea or (as we might call it) "spirit", may be composed or called forth by the use of those things which are harmonious with it, and express particular parts of its nature.*
>
> Aleister Crowley[1]

The basic contention of the Kabbalah is that the whole of the universe is a unity and that everything in creation is related to everything else. Moreover, everything that exists can be related to the planets and the signs of the Zodiac, to the letters of the Hebrew alphabet, to precious stones, living creatures, flowers and plants and to the gods and spiritual powers of all faiths. It is the most complete and the most elaborately worked out system of correspondences in the world.

The easiest way to approach this mystical system is by way of the Tree of the Sephiroth (see Figure 8.1 on page 108). This is a diagram of the forces which animate and control the cosmos and the life of mankind and of each individual human being. The cosmos and mankind and the individual are all regarded as being created from

---

[1] Aleister Crowley, *Magic in Theory and Practice*, first published for subscriber's only, in Paris in 1929. Reissued under the title *Crowley: Magick*, edited by John Symonds and Kenneth Grant, Routledge & Kegan Paul, London, 1973, and Samuel Weiser, Inc., York Beach ME, 1973, p. 143.

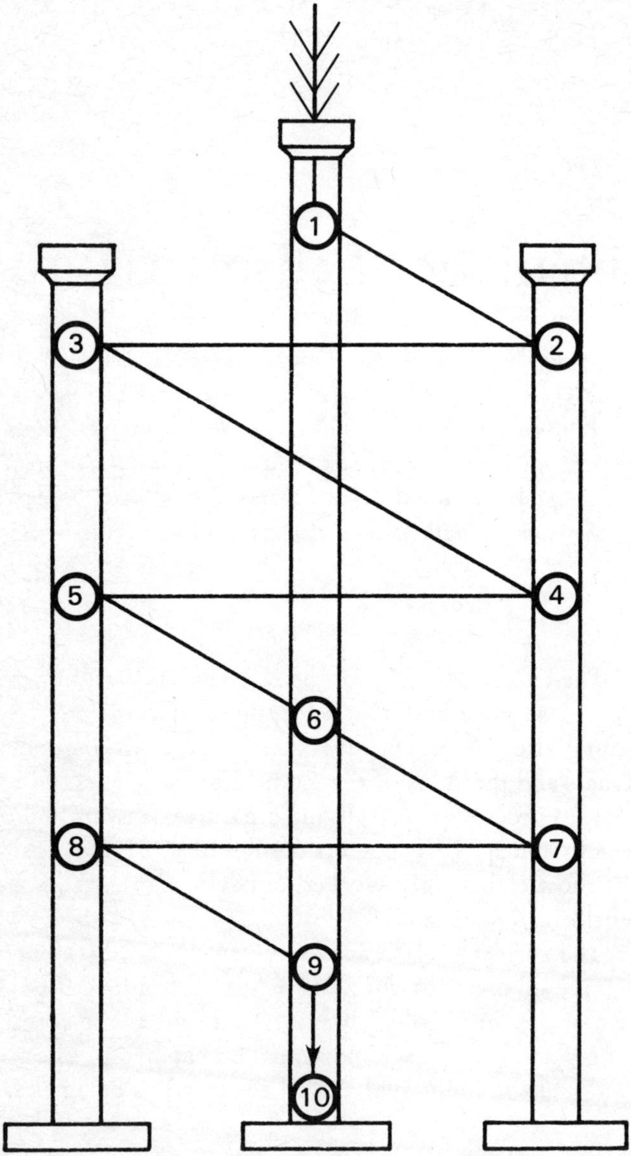

Figure 8.1 Tree of the Sephiroth.

the origin of all things by an evolutionary process. This can be shown as a descent down a ladder, or down a tree, from the ineffable to the material world of here and now. The individual and mankind must, having descended into the world we know, attempt to return up the ladder or tree and achieve unity with the spirit that is the essence of all things. This great power is unknowable by man on earth, just as the secret name of God is unknown in Mohammedan thinking. It is placed at the very top of the diagram of the tree of the Sephiroth and given the name of the Sephirah *Kether* (Sephiroth being the plural of Sephirah). From *Kether* the power flows onwards to create the second Sephirah, *Chokmah*, where what had previously been a force without direction, an unknowable and all-encompassing absolute, takes on direction. *Chokmah* has been named Wisdom and Jehovah, the first graspable idea—*Kether* is simply called the Crown. The force now moves from *Chokmah* to *Binah*, or Understanding, and the simple power of wisdom takes on form, as it were, and becomes what has also been called the Sanctifying Intelligence, the Great Sea, and the Mother. It is *Binah* which causes the second stage of evolution to begin by creating the fourth Sephirah *Chesed*. *Chesed*, although called Mercy, Love, and Majesty is, like *Chokmah*, a Sephirah of force without form; it is the fifth Sephirah, *Geburah*, which gives form to the energy of *Chesed*, just as *Binah* gave form to the energy of *Chokmah*. *Chesed* and *Geburah*, even though the latter derives from the former, are in some ways opposite; *Chesed* standing for Obedience, Law, Order, Majesty, Love, and *Geburah* for Power, Justice, and violent energy. *Chesed* is Jupiter, and *Geburah* Mars. These forces are resolved and balanced in the sixth Sephirah, *Tiphareth*, which provides a vision of the harmony of things, and which is associated with the very limit of human apprehension of spiritual truth, and therefore with the crucifixion of Christ. *Tiphareth* is indeed the highest spiritual state which a man may reach, and it is also therefore symbolized by the Sun, by a king, a child, a sacrificed god.

We have now, in the "downward flow" of the force of life, reached the spiritual experience of man, though not yet his sensual experience. The four remaining Sephiroth are those available to human experience and are called the Four Lower Sephiroth. The seventh Sephirah, *Netzach,* is called Victory, and symbolized by a beautiful naked woman. It is a vision of beauty in triumph and only one stage "down" from the complete harmony of *Tiphareth*. If this force is used positively it presents the virtues of unselfishness and love; if it is perverted it presents lust and greed. It can also be regarded as the Sephirah in which the individual experiences intuitively and psychically; in this it is opposed to the eighth Sephirah, *Hod*, which is the Sephirah associated with human reason and intelligence, and one of whose symbols is Mercury, the messenger. It represents truthfulness and, therefore, if misused, falsehood. The ninth Sephirah, *Yesod*, brings the two previous ones into harmony and is called The Foundation, for we have now reached, on the downward path, the Sephirah which is the basis of human experience, and also the first step on the upward path to illumination. *Yesod* combines both great strength and independence of judgment with a certain fluidity and restlessness. It is the stuff of life as experienced by the whole human being, the intellectual, sensual, and spiritual creature. It may be the stuff of that energy we see in auras or as the result of Kirlian photography. It is indeed the place of magical powers and also of magical confusions.

The tenth and last Sephirah on the downward evolutionary path is *Malkuth*, the Kingdom, which is life itself, sensual and intellectual existence. It is the earth we know. It is regarded as the end of the "fall" from *Kether*. It is also, however, the condition from which each of us starts to move towards *Tephireth*, towards "God," towards illumination, returning upwards on either the middle path from *Malkuth* through *Yesod* to *Tephiroth*, the path of meditation and illumination, or by a more indirect route through *Hod* or through *Netzach*.

This evolutionary process is to be seen firstly as an account of the creation and evolution of the universe we know, or think we know. Secondly, it must be seen as the creation of each individual. It must be seen, too, as a map of all the powers, knowable and unknowable, affecting us, for *Malkuth* is affected by all the previous Sephiroth. It must be seen as a map of the route towards social, personal, even national, development, and evolution "back" up the tree. The Tree, indeed, is a map that applies not only to man, but also to all other forms of life, known to us or only guessed at.

It now becomes clear that since the Tree is a map of everything that is, then everything that is must have its place on the Tree, and must fit perfectly into the pattern and into the qualities that the Sephiroth embody, and the powers of which they are composed. This is the case according to Kabbalists. All the gods and named spirits, all the archangels and angels, of all religions have their place on the Tree. All the religious systems—and especially Christianity, Judaism, Hebraism, the Greek Mysteries and the Egyptian religion—fit the pattern. Indeed, even the world of so called inanimate matter can be seen in relationship to this extraordinary design.

This being the case, the "correspondences" we have so far been observing between metals, planets, precious stones, plants and so forth can be regarded as part of one all-comprehensive system of thought and belief, one pattern. The system of correspondences was worked out most fully by Aleister Crowley and can be found in his book *777 and Other Qabalistic Writings*[2], where it occupies, together with the necessary commentaries and appendices, 155 pages. We obviously cannot repeat all this information here. We can, however, point out that once this system is recognized it causes the whole of daily experiences to be regarded as an interplay of forces which have their place in a cosmic structure and which all have powerful significance.

The kabbalistic system does not explain everything, of course, and many talismans have only an oblique relationship to it. It does, however, enable us to see where, in the system of things, talismanic power may rest. It is in the energy of *Yesod*, the Sephirah of the Moon, that we find on our diagram that balance of strength and fluidity, that energy field, which is the stuff of life and which is to be seen as the energy field of talismanic magic of all kinds. Even the "found" talisman and those we have called "organic" can be fitted into places upon the tree. As everything in existence, spiritual or material, has a place in its system, the Kabbalah is inevitably extremely complex, and its complexity has multiplied over the

---

[2]Aleister Crowley, *777 and Other Qabalistic Writings*, Samuel Weiser, Inc., York Beach ME, 1973. This volume is completely devoted to correspondences and the necessary commentaries.

centuries so that it is liable to take a student many years to learn all its various aspects. In this book, however, we do not need to explore more than some basic ideas, in order to understand the principles upon which kabbalistic talismans are made.

Firstly, it is necessary to understand that kabbalism includes astrology, and the kabbalistic talismans are therefore often based upon the need to call upon planetary powers. The planets, according to the kabbalists, are not simple forces. They include both Intelligences and Spirits—sometimes called Demons. The Intelligences are wholly beneficial; the spirits are pure power which may be used for good or for bad purposes. As a consequence of this, some occult practitioners have made use of the kabbalah for selfish and destructive ends, calling upon the powers in their dark rather than their beneficial aspects.

Secondly, we must understand that in kabbalism every letter in the Hebrew alphabet, and there are twenty-two of them, has a numerical value (see Table 8.1 on page 118). Thus it is possible to write words as numbers and numbers as words. Not only do the letters have numerical value, however, they also have symbolic significance, so that a name, or a word, can have an esoteric meaning in addition to its ordinary one. The Hebrew letter Beth (the equivalent of our B) for example, signifies ambition, intellectual activity, and science, has a numerical value 2, and corresponds to the first trump of the Tarot, the Magician (or Juggler) which in its turn symbolizes the beginnings of conscious life in the child, and the path between Kether and Binah on the Tree of the Sephiroth. It also corresponds with the Egyptian gods Thoth and Cynocephalus, Hermes (or Mercury), the swallow, ibis and ape, vervain, marjolane, herb mercury, opal, agate, the perfumes sandal, mace, storax, and the color yellow. Because it corresponds with the planet Mercury, it also corresponds with all the symbols associated with the planet. The word "Beth" also means "House."

Because the letters themselves, one by one, provide the inner meaning of words, any combination of the same letters has the same inner meaning. Consequently, by juggling the letters around, making anagrams, one can gain further insights into the word's total significance. Moreover, in such a rearrangement, the numerical value of the word remains unaltered, and this is considered important. Another way of discovering the inner meanings of words and their correspondences depends entirely upon making use of their numerical equivalents. This is called *Gematria*. The method is to convert the letters of the word into numbers, add them together, and then discover another word whose letters, when changed into numbers, add up to the same figure. This has been used by many scholars of the kabbalah in studying scripture. Richard Cavendish provides a number of interesting examples of this use. He tells us:

> When Abraham was on the plains of Mamre, Genesis says "and lo three men stood by him". The Hebrew words for 'and lo three men' add to 701. The words for 'these are Michael, Gabriel and Raphael' also add to 701, so it was deduced that the three men were really the three archangels. 'Shiloh shall come' means 'the Messiah' shall come, because Shiloh and Messiah both add to 358. . . . The ladder which Jacob saw reaching from earth to heaven is Sinai, because both *sulam* (ladder) and Sinai total 130; the law revealed from Sinai is the ladder from heaven to earth. A striking example of a genuine use of this type of code in the Old Testament comes from the Book of Daniel in which the identity of the Seleucid king Antiochus IV Epiphanes is cloaked under the name Nebuchadnezzar, probably because the Hebrew letters of both names add to 423.[3]

Gematria is not used simply to interpret scripture. It can be used "in reverse" as it were, in order to interpret numbers. Thus, Cavendish tells us, "the number 13 means 'love of unity,' because the words for 'love' and 'unity' both total 13." A surprisingly accurate discovery of gematria is that a normal pregnancy should last exactly 271 days because the letters of the word for pregnancy (*herayon*) add up to 271.

The most famous problem in gematria is, of course, that of the Great Beast whose number is 666, which appears in Revelations. There have been many solutions to this problem. A scholar called Peter Bungus once said that it referred to Martin Luther; Luther

---

[3]Richard Cavendish, *The Black Arts*, Pan Books, Picador edition, 1977, pp. 135-136. Used by permission.

Table 8.1 The Hebrew Alphabet: Some Correspondences

Hebrew Symbol	Name of Letter	English Equivalent	Meaning of Letter	Numerical Equivalent
א	Aleph	A	Ox	1
ב	Beth	B	House	2
ג	Gimel	G	Camel	3
ד	Daleth	D	Door	4
ה	He	H or E	Window	5
ו	Vau	U, V, W	Nail	6
ז	Zain	Z	Sword	7
ח	Cheth	Ch	Fence	8
ט	Teth	T	Serpent	9
י	Yod	Y + J	Hand	10
כ	Kaph	K	Palm	20 or 500
ל	Lamed	L	Ox Goad	30
מ	Mem	M	Water	40 or 600
נ	Nun	N	Fish	50 or 700
ס	Samekh	S	Prop	60
ע	Ayin	O	Eye	70
פ	Pe	O	Mouth	80 or 800
צ	Tzaddi	Tz	Fishhook	90 or 900
ק	Quoph	soft K	Back of Head	100
ר	Resh	R	Head	200
ש	Shin	Sh	Tooth	300
ת	Tau	soft T	Egyptian Tau	400

responded by saying it referred to the number of years in which the church had been ruled by Popes. Other people have, with rather suspect ingenuity, identified the beast as Napoleon, Caligula, and Nero. Aleister Crowley decided that it referred to himself. Perhaps the most ingenious, and possibly the most intellectually acceptable, is the interpretation of Robert Graves who does not use Gematria but another Kabbalistic method of interpretation and word transformation called *Notarikon*.

Notarikon consists of making either a phrase or a new word by putting together the first or the last letters of the original phrase, or of taking the constituent letters of a word or phrase and using them as the initial or final letters of a new statement. Graves used Notarikon on 666 by suggesting that, the latin for 666 being DCLXVI, it could be expanded to read *Domitius Caesar Legatos Xti Violenter Inerfecit*, or "Domitius Caesar violently killed the envoys of Christ." Domitius was the original name of Nero.[4] Other examples of Notarikon are the translation of ICTHUS, fish, into Iesos CHristos THeou Uios Soter, "Jesus Christ, the Son of God, the Savior," which we have already noted. Richard Cavendish tells us:

> The first word of the Bible—*berashith*, 'in the beginning'—has been subjected to innumerable twistings and turnings. If each of its letters are taken as the initial letters of a word, one result is 'In the beginning the Elohim (God) saw that Israel would accept the law'. Another is 'Ye shall worship my first-born, my first, whose name is Jesus', one of six examples of Notarikon which persuaded a seventeenth century Jewish cabalist to turn Christian.[5]

Gematria and Notarikon are often combined in these ingenious exercises. Sometimes, also, another method of transliteration is used called Temura. This is described most clearly by Aleister Crowley in *777 and Other Qabalistic Writings*:

> Temura is permutation. According to certain rules, one letter is substituted for another letter preceding or following it in the alphabet and thus from one word another word of totally different orthography may be formed. Thus the alphabet is bent exactly in half, in the middle, and one half is put over the other; and then by changing alternately the first letter or the first two letters at the beginning of the second line, twenty-two commutations are produced. These are called the "Tables of the Combinations of TzIRVP,

---

[4]See Robert Graves, *The White Goddess*, Faber and Faber, London, 1948, pp. 340-346.
[5]Richard Cavendish, *The Black Arts*, Pan Books, Picador Edition, 1977, p. 136. Used by permission.

> Tziruph." For example's sake, I will give the method called ALBTh, Albath. Thus:-
>
> | | | | | | | | | | | |
> |---|---|---|---|---|---|---|---|---|---|---|
> | 11 | 10 | 9 | 8 | 7 | 6 | 5 | 4 | 3 | 2 | 1 |
> | K | I | T | Ch | Z | V | H | D | G | B | A |
> | M | N | S | O | P | Tz | Q | R | Sh | Th | L |
>
> Each method takes its name from the first two pairs composing it, the system of pairs of letters being the groundwork of the whole, as either letter in a pair is substituted for the other letter. Thus, by ALbath, from RVCh, Ruach, is formed DTzO, Detzau.[6]

This looks more difficult than it is unless we realize that we are dealing with the Hebrew alphabet of 22 letters and that Hebrew reads from right to left. It then becomes one of the simplest of substitution codes. There are as many methods of Temura as there are letters in the Hebrew alphabet. The others are ABGTh (which means that the two pairs on the right are written as G A). The others are AGDTh, ADBG, AHBD, AVBH, AZBV, AChBZ, ATPCh, AIBT, AKBI, ALBK, AMBL, ANBM, ASBN, AOBS, APBO, ATzBP, AQSTz, AREQ, AShBR, and AThBsh. There are, for some reason, two others, ABGD and ALBM.

There are several other methods of Temura, none of them particularly complicated and all of them familiar to anyone interested in simple kinds of codes.

Much of this may seem irrelevant to the consideration of talismans, but talismans frequently make use of words of power, and these words of power have often been formulated through the use of Gematria, Notarikon, or Temura. Moreover, many of the names of angels, spirits, and intelligences have been constructed in a similar manner. Consequently, if one wished to find the name of, or *a* name *for* the spirit of a particular place or even object, one might choose to do so using these methods. As an illustration let us take the name OTTAWA. Using Crowley's method of transliteration, which is

---

[6] Aleister Crowley, *777 and Other Qabalistic Writings*, Samuel Weiser, Inc., York Beach, ME, 1973, p. 3. Used by permission.

generally regarded as the most authoritative, we get the Hebrew letters Ayin (70), Teth (9), Aleph (1), Vau (6), Aleph (1). Some gematrists might omit the vowels because in orthodox gematria they are not taken into account, in which case we would get only Teth (9) and Vau (6). Thus we have now to find a name that adds up to either 87 or 15. The number 87 could provide the three letters Gimel (3), Peh (80), Daleth (4), which translates as GPD and, by Notarikon, could read as "God Preserve Democracy." The number 15 could result in Beth (2), Gimel (3), Yodh (10), which transliterate as BGY and could result in the word "Bogey."

This may be facetious, but if one wishes to create a talisman which uses words found specially for it, and which correspond exactly to the work the talisman is to perform, then the methods here provided will do the job. Ideally, of course, the whole of the operation should be conducted in Hebrew, as all the kabbalistic systems are based upon the language. Nevertheless, there is good precedent for adjusting the system to work with another alphabet. Modern western Numerology has developed a most effective and sophisticated system of divination from the methods used by the Greeks and Hebrews, and though this need not concern us here as it is rarely used in the making of talismans, it does suggest that when we are dealing with concepts that belong essentially in languages using the Roman Alphabet, some form of adaptation might be in order. Modern numerologists use the following table of numerical equivalents:

A:1, B:2, C:3, D:4, E:5, F:6, G:7, H:8, I:9, J:1,
K:11, L:3, M:4, N:5, O:6, P:7, Q:8, R:9, S:1, T:1,
U:3, V:22, W:5, X:6, Y:7, Z:8.

This would give us 15 as the numerical equivalent of Ottawa, and, by Gematria, we could produce the word Tome or Ties and a number of others. In dealing with the Roman Alphabet in this way, however, we must realize that it has never been deliberately organized into a system of multiple correspondences as has Hebrew, and that therefore our experiments are likely to have limited results. The Hebrew system is indeed very complex. Just as the letters have significance in themselves so do the numbers, and many talismans are made entirely from numbers. The numbers basic to all forms of numerological thinking are those from 1 to 9, for these are the basis of all later numbers, and all have importance. In the arabic alphabet, for example, the first letter of the alphabet is 1 and its significance is God. Other correspondences are 2: male and female, heaven and earth, light and dark, sun and moon, winter and summer, and indeed all pairs of this kind. 4 stands for the 4 archangels, elements, and seasons and explains why these talismans are always squares and not rectangles. 7 is particularly powerful, for it alludes to the 7 heavens, planets, and hells, and the Seven Seals and the 7 stages in the life of man as well as the seven prophets, Moses, Jesus, David, Solomon, Jacob, Adam and Muhammad, who preside over the 7 days of the week respectively.

The basic principle of talismans using numbers appears to be that the numbers, when given letter equivalents, should spell out a name of power, or, when added together, result in the numerical equivalent of a name of power or a passage of scripture. In Arab talismans it is frequent for the name chosen to be one of the ninety-nine names of God which we have already listed on page 76. Sometimes four or more names of God are chosen, according to the particular attributes of God that the talisman maker wishes to bring into mind. The sheer ingenuity of these talismans is clearly regarded as magical in itself. The amount of intellectual labor and cunning required to construct them is regarded as proof of a corresponding amount of passion, faith, and magical energy.

One talisman using the numbers 1 to 9 is of great antiquity. Although nowadays known as the Table of Saturn, (see Figure 8.2 on page 124), it is supposed to have been discovered by the Chinese Emeror Yaou inscribed on the back of a huge tortoise which appeared on the banks of the Yellow River in 2348 B.C. after a great flood. This talisman takes the form of a *Zahlenquadrat*, or magic square, in which the numbers of the vertical columns and the horizontal columns add up to the same number (15), which is also the sum of the numbers read diagonally. The table is called the eightfold path or *Patao* by the Chinese because there are eight squares surrounding the central square which is the number for man himself, 5, which is related to the 5 senses.

The Zahlenquadrat is the basis of all kabbalistic planetary talismans, where it is called a *Kamea*. The numbers are directly related to the numerical equivalent of the names of the intelligence and/or spirit of the planet, or to some other significant name. The sigil, or seal, of the planet's intelligence and spirit is made by drawing lines within the numerical squares that spell out, numerically, the correct names. The actual sign of the planet itself is basically an abstract design so contrived as to pass through all the numbers in the squares.[7]

The talisman made according to this system should have the Kamea on one side of it and the sign of the planet and the sigil (sign) of its intelligence on the other. The sigil of its spirit (or demon) may be added for extra power, but the demon's sigil should never be used without the sigil of the intelligence to control it. In addition to this one may add to the talisman the names which are associated with the planet, those of its angels and archangels, and, indeed, any other names considered relevant. These talismans should be worn as pendants, though they can also be used as brooches, belt buckles, or rings provided that the necessary attachments do not touch the actual designs.

There are differing views of the powers of these planetary talismans and some of the names are transliterated from the Hebrew in different ways by different occultists. The following, however, gives as full a picture, including variants, as seems necessary.

Saturn

Saturn's Spirit is Agiel (45), and the Demon is Zazel (45). The numbers in the Kamea add up, in toto, to 45 which is not only the number of both the spirit and the demon but also that of the full length tetragrammaton, the name of God, which can be written as YWD HA WAW HA (see Figure 8.3). The shortest form of the Tetragrammaton is YH (abbreviated from YHWH) which has the

[7]This information is gathered together from a large number of different sources, including works by Eliphas Levi, A. E. Waite, Israel Regardie and *The Key of Solomon* by Mathers. One of the more complete accounts can be found in Israel Regardie's *The Golden Dawn*, Llewellyn Publications, St. Paul, MN, 1971. This does not, however, include the Hebrew. This can be found in E. A. Wallis Budge's *Amulets and Talismans*.

ד	ט	ב
ג	ה	ז
ח	א	ו

4	9	2
3	5	7
8	1	6

Figure 8.2 Table of Saturn

numerical equivalent of 15 (Y, Yod, being 10, and H, He, being 5), and all the horizontal and vertical columns in the Kamea add up to 15 as do the diagonals. This is the oldest recorded Kamea and appears to have been in use in Sumerian times and in ancient India. This Kamea should be made of lead, which is the metal of Saturn, and on a Saturday.

Some commentators state that this talisman will bring greater ability in business and politics, and help the wearer to shoulder heavier responsibilities and duties. Others point to the medical associations of the planet, which we have already discussed, and state that the talisman protects against being killed as a consequence of poison or conspiracy. It is also a protection for women in childbirth.

ד	ט	ב
ג	ה	ז
ח	א	ו

4	9	2
3	5	7
8	1	6

Seal of the Planet — Spirit: Zazel — Intelligence: Agiel

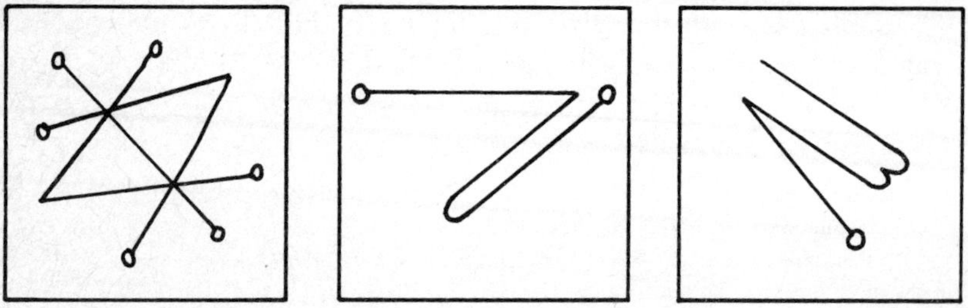

Figure 8.3 Kamea of Saturn.

ד	יד	יה	א
ט	ז	ו	יב
ה	יא	י	ח
יו	ב	ג	יג

4	14	15	1
9	7	6	12
5	11	10	8
16	2	3	13

Seal of the Planet   Spirit: Hismael   Intelligence: Yophiel

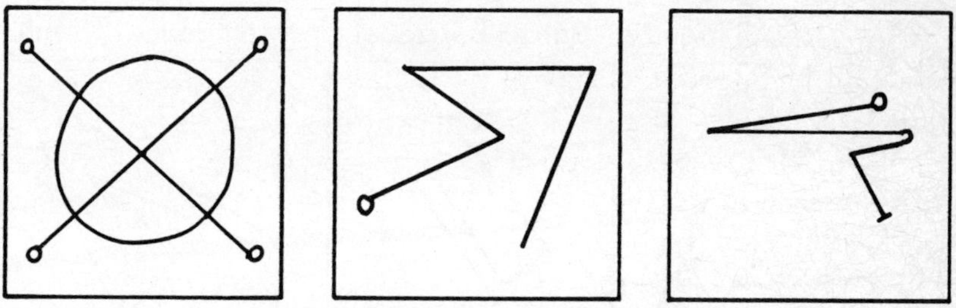

Figure 8.4 Kamea of Jupiter.

Jupiter

Jupiter's Intelligence is Yophiel (136) and the Demon is Hasmael (or Hismael) (136). The sum of all the numbers in the square is 136. When the numbers in the vertical and horizontal columns and the two diagonals are added the result is 34 which is the numerical equivalent of the Hebrew word for tin (see Figure 8.4). This talisman should be made of tin and on Thursday. According to some authorities it can also be made on coral as a protection against witchcraft.

This talisman is a protective talisman for travelers, and a help in legal and commercial negotiations. It causes sympathy in others and banishes anxiety, and also protects against accidents.

Mars

Mars' Intelligence is Graphiel (325) and the Demon is Barsabel (or Bartzabel) (325). All the numbers add up to 325, and the vertical and horizontal columns and the diagonals add up to 65

יא	כד	ז	כ	ג
ד	יב	כה	ח	יו
יז	ה	יג	כא	ט
י	יח	א	יד	כב
כג	ו	יט	ב	יה

11	24	7	20	3
4	12	25	8	16
17	5	13	21	9
10	18	1	14	22
23	6	19	2	15

Seal of the Planet

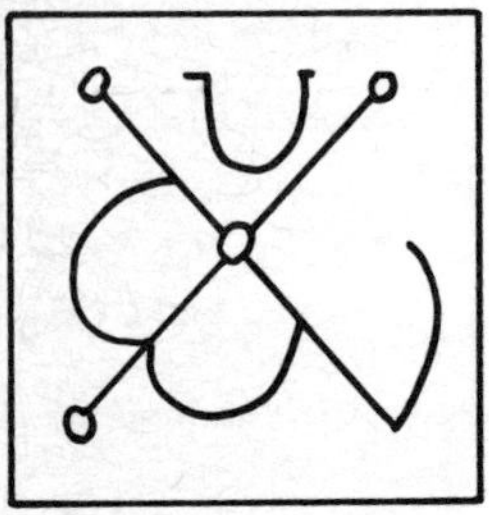

Spirit: Bartzabel

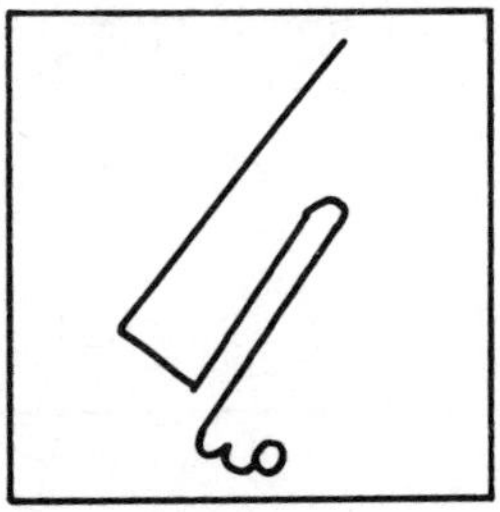

Intelligence: Graphiel

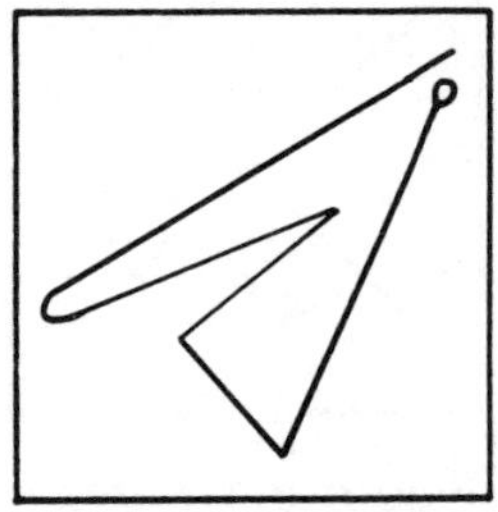

Figure 8.5 Kamea of Mars.

which is the numerical equivalent of ADNY or ADONAY, one of the names of God. (See Figure 8.5). The talisman should be made of iron and on a Thursday. It protects against enemies, and assists the wearer in matters connected with machinery. It also increases the wearer's strength and physical courage.

Sun

The Sun's Intelligence is Nakiel (or Nakhiel) (111) and the Demon is Sorath (666). The overall total of the figures is 666, and the vertical and horizontal columns and the diagonals add up to 111 as shown in Figure 8.6. Six hundred and sixty-six is, of course, the powerful number of the "Great Beast" of Revelations. The number 111, however, a triple unity is even more powerful. The talisman should be made of gold and on a Sunday. It strengthens the wearer's confidence and powers of leadership.

ו	לב	ג	לד	לה	א
ז	יא	כז	כח	ח	ל
כד	יד	יו	יה	כג	יט
יג	כ	כב	כא	יז	יח
כה	כט	י	ט	כו	יב
לו	ה	לג	ד	כ	לא

6	32	3	34	35	1
7	11	27	28	8	30
19	14	16	15	23	24
18	20	22	21	17	13
25	29	10	9	26	12
36	5	33	4	2	31

Seal of the Planet*

Spirit: SORATH

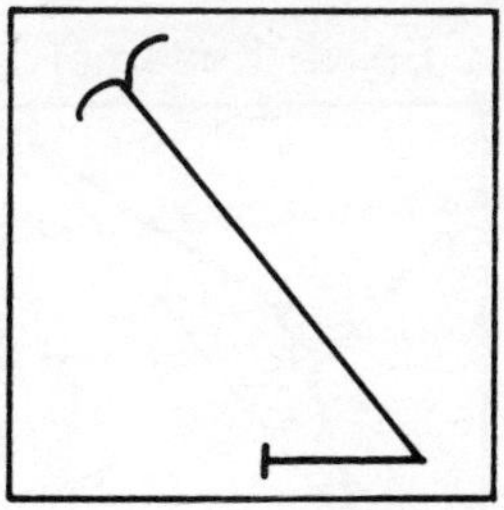

Intelligence: Nakhiel

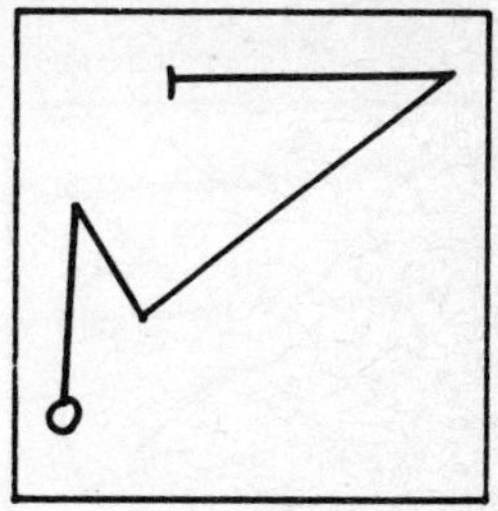

Figure 8.6 Kamea of the Sun *(Sol).* Note* that the Sun is called a "planet" by many astrologers. The term was coined because it was easier to say the "ten planets" when referring to the celestial bodies, rather than the correct "eight planets and two luminaries." Astrologers know, however, that both the Sun and the Moon are not planets.

Venus

The Intelligence of Venus is Hagiel (49), and the Demon is Kedemel (175). There is an additional intelligence in the form of a choir of angels named the Beni Seraphim. The numbers in the squares represent Hagiel by running from 1 to 9. The columns horizontally, vertically and diagonally add up to 175 which is not only the number of Kedemel but also the number of the Hebrew (Sodh-Mny) for "Secret council of the goddess Meny," Meny being a name for Venus. The total for all the numbers is 1,225 which is the number of the Beni Seraphim, which are the highest order of angels,

כב	מז	יו	מא	י	לה	ד
ה	כג	מח	יז	מב	יא	כט
ל	ו	כד	מט	יח	לו	יב
יג	לא	ז	כה	מג	יט	לז
לח	יד	לב	א	כו	מד	כ
כא	לט	ח	לג	ב	כז	מה
מו	יה	מ	ט	לד	ג	כח

22	47	16	41	10	35	4
5	23	48	17	42	11	29
30	6	24	49	18	36	12
13	31	7	25	43	19	37
38	14	32	1	26	44	20
21	39	8	33	2	27	45
46	15	40	9	34	3	28

Seal of the Planet Spirit: Kedemel Intelligence: Hagiel

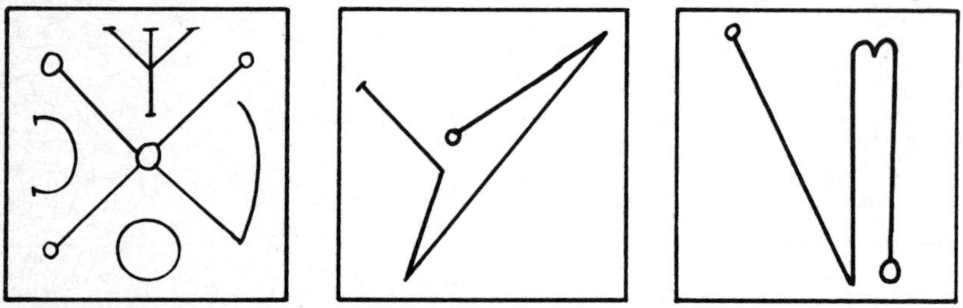

Figure 8.7 Kamea of Venus.

and angels of love, light, and fire. There are 4 seraphim according to most authorities and the leader of them has been named variously as Michael, Seraphiel, Johoel, and Metatron. Satan is supposed to have been their leader before his fall. This talisman should be made of copper and on a Friday. It preserves marital happiness and can transform dislike to affection. It protects women from cancer, and everyone from poison. It also helps with all social relationships and in money matters. (See Figure 8.7.)

Mercury

Mercury's Intelligence is Tiriel (260) and the Demon is Taphthartharath (2080). The horizontal, vertical and diagonal columns add up to 260 which is the number of Tiriel and also the number of the consonants in the Hebrew for "Star of Living

ח	נח	נט	ה	ד	סב	סג	א
מט	יה	יד	נב	נג	יא	י	נו
מא	כג	כב	מד	מה	יט	יח	מח
לב	לד	לה	כט	כח	לח	לט	כה
מ	כו	כז	לז	לו	ל	לא	לג
יז	מז	מו	כ	כא	מג	מב	כד
ט	נה	נד	יב	יג	נא	נ	יו
סד	ב	ג	סא	ס	ו	ז	נז

8	58	59	5	4	62	63	1
49	15	14	52	53	11	10	56
41	23	22	44	45	19	18	48
32	34	35	29	28	38	39	25
40	26	27	37	36	30	31	33
17	47	46	20	21	43	42	24
9	55	54	12	13	51	50	16
64	2	3	61	60	6	7	57

Seal of the Planet

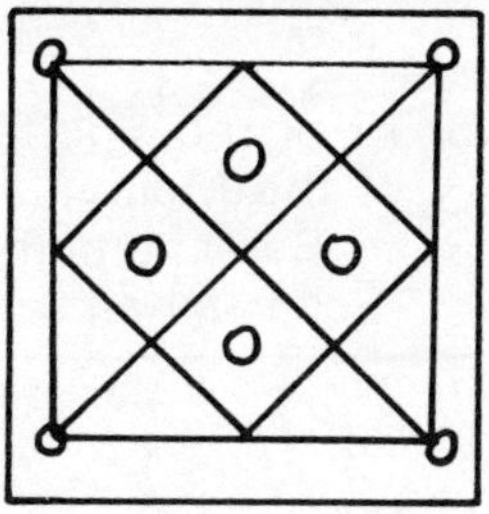

Spirit: Taphthartharath

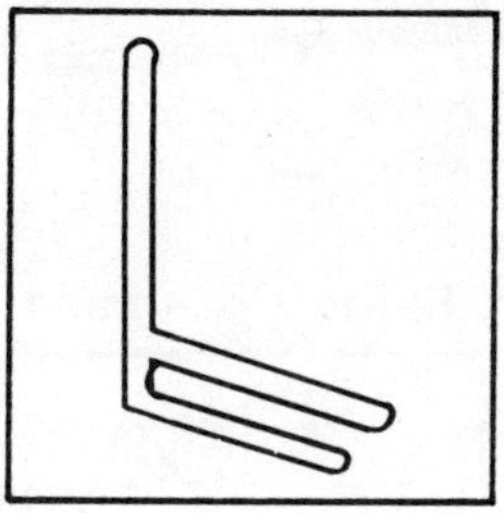

Intelligence: Ririel

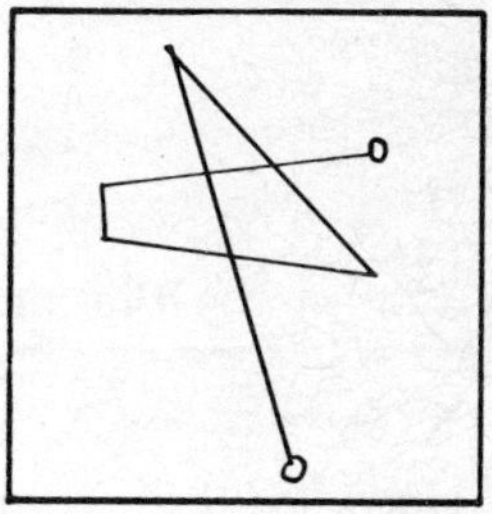

Figure 8.8 Kamea of Mercury.

Silver" (kokab kesef hayyim). All the numbers add up to 2,080. The talisman (see Figure 8.8) should be made of tin and on a Wednesday though it can also be made of aluminum, silver, or platinum. It helps in all matters to do with commerce, and if buried under the threshold of a shop, or even placed above the door, it will attract customers. It preserves its wearers from madness and epilepsy, and from death by murder. If placed beneath the pillow at night it can bring prophetic dreams. It is also good as a protection while traveling.

Moon

The Moon's Intelligence (Figure 8.9) is Malka Betharshesim (or Malcah Betarshisim ve-ad ruachoth ha-schedralim)

לז	עח	כט	ע	כא	סב	יג	נד	ה
ו	לח	עט	ל	עא	כב	סג	יד	מו
מז	ז	לט	פ	לא	עב	כג	נה	יה
יו	מח	ח	מ	פא	לב	סד	כד	נו
נז	יז	מט	ט	מא	עג	לג	סה	כה
כו	נח	יח	נ	א	מב	עד	לד	סו
סז	כז	נט	י	נא	ב	מג	עה	לה
לו	סח	יט	ס	יא	נב	ג	מד	עו
עז	כח	סט	כ	סא	יב	נג	ד	מה

37	78	29	70	21	62	13	54	5
6	38	79	30	71	22	63	14	46
47	7	39	80	31	72	23	55	15
16	48	8	40	81	32	64	24	56
57	17	49	9	41	73	33	65	25
26	58	18	50	1	42	74	34	66
67	27	59	10	51	2	43	75	35
36	68	19	60	11	52	3	44	76
77	28	69	20	61	12	53	4	45

Seal of the Planet

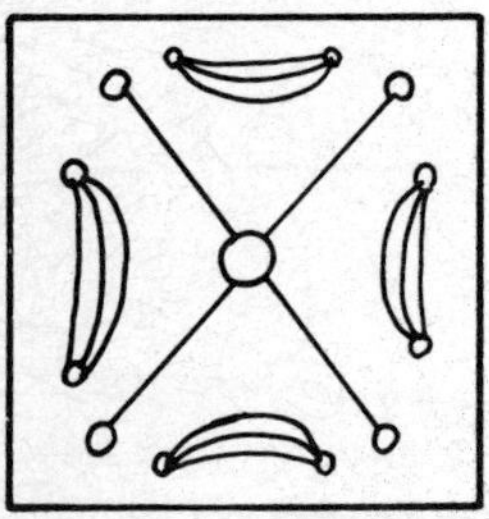

Spirit: Chashmod

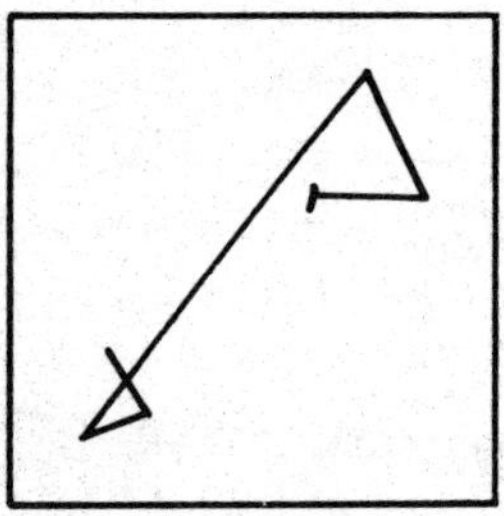

Spirit of the Spirits of the Moon: Shad Barschemoth Schartathan

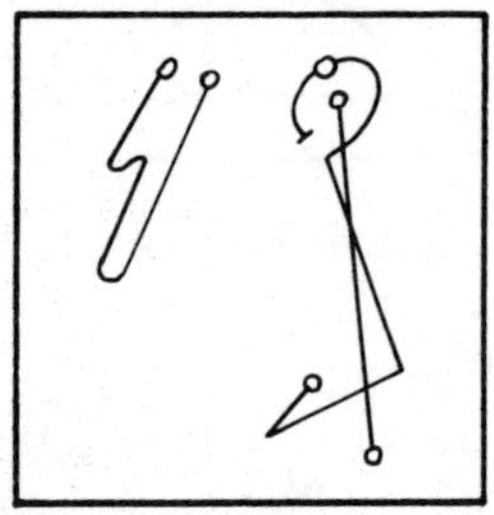

Intelligence of the Intelligences of the Moon: Malcha Betarshisim Ve-ad Ruachoth Ha-Schechalim

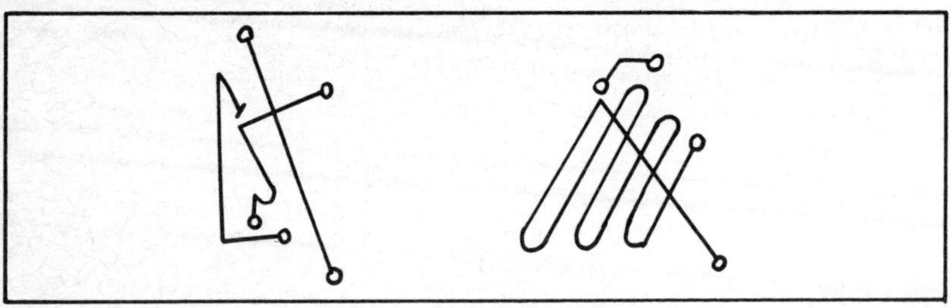

Figure 8.9 Kamea of the Moon *(Luna).*

(3321), and the Demon is Hasmoday (or Chasmodai) (369). The Demons of the moon have a demon of their own named Shedbarshemoth Sharthathan (or Shad Barshemoth Hschartathan) (3321). The numbers in the horizontal and vertical columns and diagonally add up to 369, which is the number not only of Hasmoday but also of the consonants in the Hebrew for "golden horn" (keren ha-zahab). All the figures add up to 3,321. It should be made of silver and on a Monday. This talisman helps in all domestic matters and in anything to do with plant growth and the care of animals.

All these talismans should not only be made on the appropriate day, but at a time when the moon is waxing, and at an hour ruled by the planet when the moon is in good aspect to it. One authority suggests that the appropriate hours in all cases are from midday to 1 P.M., from 7 to 8 P.M., from 2-3 A.M. and from 9-10 A.M. the next day. This seems, on the face of it, to be a little too easy.

The talismans described here are not the only planetary talismans prescribed by tradition, though they are the most complicated and intellectually interesting. Another series of seven is described in considerable detail by Eliphas Levi in his *Rituel de la Haute Magie* (1856).[8]

The basic pattern of these talismans is a circle of metal on one side of whch is engraved a pentagram, a five pointed star made of two triangles, with two points at the bottom and one at the top. To place it or think of it upside down with the two "horns" at the top is to court disaster. This pentagram should be accompanied by the signs of the planets, preferably not the conventional ones but others, these being for the sun a circle, the moon a crescent, (pointing to the left), Mars a sword, Venus a G, Jupiter a crown, Mercury a caduceus and Saturn a scythe. These should be placed outside the pentagram design itself, except for the sign that applies to the particular planet involved. On the reverse side of the talisman

---

[8]This title, translated into English by A. E. Waite, and called *Transcendental Magic: Its Doctrine and Ritual*, is published in the UK by Rider & Co., and in the USA by Samuel Weiser, Inc.

the shield of Solomon or six pointed star composed of two triangles should be engraved.

It is this reverse side which makes the talisman particular to a given planet. The emblem of the planet should be engraved in the center of the design: for the Sun a human figure, for the Moon a chalice, for Mercury a dog's head, for Jupiter an eagle's head, for Mars a lion's head, for Venus a dove's head, for Saturn the head of either a goat or a bull. The names of the seven angels of the planet should be added and written in Hebrew, or Arabic, or one of the kabbalistic and magical alphabets which have been created for such purposes. There is some disagreement over which angels govern which planet, but the consensus appears to be that Raphael governs the Sun; Aniel, Venus; Michael, Mercury; Gabriel, the Moon; Zaphiel, Saturn; Zadkiel, Jupiter; and Camael, Mars. The metals used for these talismans are the same as for the others I have described.

It is not, of course, enough to construct these talismans. They have to be imbued with power, to be consecrated.

Chapter 9

The Consecration of Talismans

The virtue of consecrations chiefly consists in two things, viz. *the power of the person consecrating, and the virtue of the prayer by which the consecration is made.*
For in the person consecrating, there is required firmness, constancy, and holiness of life; and that the consecrator himself shall, with a firm and indubitable faith, believe the virtue, power, and effect thereof.

Francis Barrett
The Magus

In the making of talismans, we face three tasks. We must make, or find, or buy, an object proper to our purpose. We must purify it by cleansing it of all associations and transfer energies that we do not wish it to possess. And we must give it the power and intent we wish it to have by means of some kind of blessing, or consecration.

The subject of purification and consecration is of such importance that we will deal with it here as a separate chapter. The principle behind consecration is simple: that which carries conviction is correct. Some may choose to purify their talismans by means of complex established rituals, such as those used by Eliphas Levi, and we shall take a look at the nature of some of these rituals later in this chapter. Others may decide that a simpler method will do. The important thing is to be absolutely convinced of the efficacy of your procedures.

There are numerous ways to purify a talisman. It can be done by blessing it in the name of the powers that carry most conviction to you, while symbolically washing it. In other words, one may imitate baptism, which is, of course, itself a purification rite. Or you may hold the talisman up to the four quarters of the heaven and invoke purification by the four elements. You may choose simply to place it over incense which will, you feel, banish all previous associations it may have. Or you may lay it out in the garden under a glass dome on a night of the full moon, asking the moonlight to purify it. Indeed, as long as whatever you do has strong connections with ideas of washing clean, or making bright with light, or banishing by means of fire and smoke, or making whole by subjecting it to an expression of cosmic unity, you cannot go far wrong.

After purification comes consecration. This can take many forms. There are elaborate rituals available as we shall see, and you may like to use one of these or even create one of your own, or you may take other routes to your goal. One such is to place your talisman for a time in a box with objects that are already charged with the correct energy or that are symbolic of it. If you have created a talisman to bring wealth, for example, you might place it in a box with gold and silver coins or other symbols of money. This is using the principle of energy transference, or of psychic contagion. If this is not possible, then you can follow the principle of morning and evening concentration to charge the talisman as you would charge a battery. To do this, take the talismanic object and hold it in your hand and concentrate upon its protective qualities. Hold it for as long as you can keep up the concentration. Then place it in a wrapping of silk or in a special place reserved for it. Do not treat it casually. Charge it again at the next opportunity. It is a good thing to do this early in the morning, for after sleep the deep mind is always sensitized. Late at night when the deep mind is ready for dreams is also a suitable time. If this can also be done at the time of the waxing moon or the night of a full moon, so much the better.[1]

---

[1]It's important to mention that you should not let anyone but yourself handle this object, unless it is a person whom you wholly trust and whose blessing would reinforce its power. Here one must be very careful. A person may love you deeply and be willing to go along with your "fantasies," but inwardly be entirely skeptical. It is, on the whole, best to keep these things to yourself.

On the whole, however, the consecration that is the most effective will be one which causes the talisman maker to make a special effort and to do something which he would not normally do. By putting on special clothes, or using incantations, or by taking the talisman to a mountain top or to a particular place, or putting it at the feet of certain statue, the talisman maker is expressing in physical terms the concentrated power of his intent, and the physical acts he performs remind him continually of the intent. It is hard to lay down any general code of practice for consecrating talismans, as each talisman maker must have his or her own particular and individual one, but here are some suggestions:

1. Do not wear much clothing. The talisman should be bathed in as much of your energy field as possible. If total nudity embarrasses you, then wear a simple white shift or a pair of pajamas—anything in which you feel physically comfortable and unconstricted.

2. Perform your consecration in a tidy room. In a tidy room everything is in its allotted place and therefore the many energy fields are not fighting each other, or even more important, are not felt to be fighting each other by the talisman maker. Whatever tensions occur in the room should be related directly to the act of consecration and be a positive part of that act. If the room can be bare except for what is needed for the act of consecration so much the better. A totally bare room, however, may in some instances inhibit as much as it helps.

3. If you are using a table of any kind make sure that it is clean and decent and if there is anything on it, it should be associated with your consecration. Flowers of whatever you feel to be a sympathetic color may assist you, as my other objects which you feel to have a talismanic power supporting your own intent. Such symbolic objects as sea shells, colored stones, and candles can be used. White candles are preferred, but here again you should go by your own individual reading of color symbolism. Don't use muddy colors and avoid mixed ones unless they are radiant and vibrant. A bowl of water may help some, and a container of salt and oil may also help. Again we are here subject to the vagaries of the individual sensibility. The table must not, however, be cluttered. I do not believe that many people can carry out an act of consecration

successfully if the table looks like a cross between a curio shop and a harvest festival.

4. You may, if you like, use music as an accompaniment. This is less to support your concentration positively than to block out noises from elsewhere. The music should therefore be relatively unemphatic unless, of course, you have a piece of music that means so much to you personally and has for you such power that it can help you to do the work.

5. Obviously, if you are not alone, whoever is with you must take part in the conscration wholeheartedly, either by joining in whatever words you use, or by handing you what you need. It is best, however, to do the work alone, unless your companion or companions are totally at one with you and fully understand and sympathize with what you are doing.

6. If at all possible, do not use that room again for any other purpose until the day following, and leave the talisman in the room after it has been consecrated. It may be left in its protective silk wrapping of whatever color is appropriate, or in its special box, or it may be left out on the table. But it should not be taken away and used until the night is over.

7. Finally, when the consecration is finished and you leave the room, remove your clothing (if you were wearing any) straight away and put it aside for the next occasion or into the laundry. If you were naked you should put on some clothing in order to signify the end of your task.

All the above presumes that the consecration of the talisman is a quite separate operation from the making, or buying, or finding of it. If you do in fact manufacture the talisman, then it may be difficult to do so in the same room as you consecrate it, or with the same accompaniment. I foresee trouble if you attempt to pour molten lead into a mould while unprotected by clothing, for example. Nevertheless, while making your kamea or your pentagram or your mandala, do wear some special article of clothing, and do it with careful regard to the environment in which you are working, and, of course, concentrate upon your intent the whole of the time you are working. In this way you will build intent into the object before the time for consecration comes and it will be that much more effective.

Eliphas Levi has written extensively about the consecration of talismans, and has made the whole operation very complicated indeed. He states that first of all the talisman maker is required to have an altar upon which is a tripod of sacred fire, and the altar and the tripod must be garlanded. Before the altar must be a carpet of a specific kind, and the magician must wear robes of a particular color together with various crowns, bracelets and rings. The altar must also be perfumed. The details are as follows:

Sunday. The operation should take place between midnight and eight a.m. or from three p.m. to ten p.m. The robe must be purple with bracelets and a crown of gold. The garlands must be of laurel, heliotrope and sunflowers, and the perfumes must be cinnamon, saffron, red sandalwood, and strong incense. The magician must wear a gold ring and stand on a carpet made of a lion skin, and there must be also—it is not clear whether on the altar or in his hand—fans made of the feathers of sparrows. This is the day to make talismans of the sun.

Monday. No time for the operation is given, but the robe must be white with silver embroidery, and decorated with a collar of three layers made of pearls, crystals, and selenite. He must wear a crown covered in a piece of yellow silk on which the Hebrew monogram of Gabriel is embroidered in silver. The perfumes to be used are white sandalwood, camphor, amber, aloes, and pulverized seed of cucumber, and the garlands must be of mugwort, moonwort and yellow ranunculus. This is the day to make moon talismans.

Tuesday. The robes must be the color of flame or rust or blood, and belted with steel. Steel bracelets should be worn. The crown must have gold bound round it, and the ring must be of steel with an amethyst in it. The garlands must be of absinth and rue. No perfumes are mentioned, for some reason. This is the day to make a talisman of Mars and a day, too, to make a talisman to assist in vengeance.

Wednesday. The robes must be green or variously colored, and the magician should wear a necklace made of pearls which are enclosed together with Mercury in glass beads. The jewel for the day is agate. The perfumes must be benzoin, mace, and storax, and the garlands should be of narcissus, lily, herb-mercury, fumitory and marjoram. This is the day for making the talisman of Mercury.

Thursday. The robes should be scarlet, and the magician should wear upon his forehead a brass plaque engraved with the sign for the spirit of Jupiter and the words GIARAR, BETHOR, SAMGADIEL.[2] The magician should wear an emerald or a sapphire in a ring. The perfumes for the day are ambergris, incense, balm, grain of paradise, macis and saffron, and the garlands must be made of oak, poplar, pomegranate and fig leaves. This is the day to make the talisman of Jupiter.

Friday. The robes must be colored sky blue, and the room should be decorated with hangings of green and of rose. The ornaments should be of highly polished copper, and the magician should wear a turquoise ring. The crown and the belt clasps should be of lapis lazuli and beryl. The fans must be made of swans' feathers, and the talisman maker should wear a copper pendant engraved with the name Anael, who is one of the seven angels of creation and who has particular charge over Venus, and also the words AVEENA VADELILITH.[3] Friday is, of course, the day for making talismans of Venus.

Saturday. The robes must be black or very dark brown, and embroidered in black and orange silk. A lamina of lead engraved with the sign of Saturn and the words ALMALEC, APHIEL, ZARAHIEL must be worn around the neck. The ring should bear black onyx on which the double head of Janus should be engraved during the hours dominated by Saturn. The required perfumes are diagridium, scammony, alum, sulfur, and assafoetida, and the

---

[2] I am unable to track down Giarar and Samgadiel, but Bethor is a ruling angel of Jupiter.

[3] This phrase is intended to banish Lilith, who is regarded as being the evil angel of Friday, and one of the most powerful of all evil powers, and to welcome the spirit of Venus. The first word AVEENA is a conflation of the two words AVE (Hail, or Welcome) and VENUS, and the second is made up of the two words VADE (Go, and Begone!) and LILITH. This kind of conflation and distortion is common in talismanic practice.

garlands should be made of ash, cypress, and hellebore. This is, of course, the day to make the talisman of Saturn.

In 1870, fifteen years after the appearance of Eliphas Levi's *Transcendental Magic*, Paul Christian published his *History and Practice of Magic*[4] and in his book he included all but one of the above planetary talismans according to Levi's formulae with one or two errors. He changed the consecration process, however. He made no mention of altars, vestments, rings, hangings and fans. He stated simply that the talisman should be held over the smoke of a fire made in an earthenware pot, the fire being composed of materials appropriate to the nature of each planet. For this perfuming he makes use of most of the materials listed by Eliphas Levi. He states that the talisman of Saturn should be perfumed with the result of alum, asafoetida, scampony, and sulfur being burned in a fire of cypress, ash and black hellebore. The talisman for Jupiter requires frankincense, ambergris, balsam, cardamon, saffron, and mace to be burned on a fire of oak, poplar, fig and pomegranate wood. The talisman of Mars he treats more perfunctorily, merely subjecting it to the smell of desiccated absinth (sic) and rue. The talisman of the Sun needs a recipe of cinnamon, frankincense, saffron, red sandalwood, burned with laurel and the dried stalks of heliotrope. The talisman of Venus requires a simpler procedure. It is simply held in the fumes of a fire of olive wood in which violets and roses are burned. The talisman of Mercury requires benzoin, mace and storax to be burned on a fire of dried lily and narcissus stalks, marjoram and fumitory. The talisman of the Moon requires the perfume of white sandalwood, camphor, aloes, amber and pounded cucumber seeds burned on a fire of dried stalks of artemisia, selenotrope and ranunculus.

In all these cases, the earthenware vessel should not have been used previously and should be broken and buried afterwards. The talismans should, according to Paul Christian, be placed in silk sachets and hung around the neck, the colors of the sachets to be of the following: Saturn, black; Jupiter, sky-blue; Mars, red; Sun, pale yellow; Venus, green or pink; Mercury, purple; Moon, white.

---

[4] *The History and Practice of Magic*, translated by James Kirkup and Julian Shaw, was reprinted by the Citadel Press, Secaucus, NJ, 1972.

A.E. Waite's *The Occult Sciences* (published in 1923) follows the method of consecration devised by Paul Christian, but adds to it his own description of the actual ritual of consecration given by Eliphas Levi. To go into detail here of the elaborate ceremonial ritual of Levi would take us too far from our purpose, which is to survey the talismans themselves.

Now it is time to look back at what we have seen of esoteric talismans and their making, and to comment upon it all. Firstly it seems clear that while the kameas are laborious to construct they are not absurdly so, and that the planetary talismans of Levi, Christian, and Waite are not particularly difficult to make either. The consecrating of the talismans appears to be the difficult part and if anyone attempted to follow the rituals of Eliphas Levi in full he would need a fat bank account to purchase even the basic materials for his clothes and equipment. He would also need a very well stocked cupboard of herbs and perfumes and an equally well stocked garden. Indeed, it's clear that these requirements present the talisman maker with obstacles that may be insuperable. That some of them are intended to present difficulties is obvious. How can one possibly construct a necklace of glass beads with Mercury and pearls within them? And who, on a day in winter, will be able to find the materials for most of the garlands? Can talismans only be made in the summer, then, or when the appropriate plants are in bloom? Moreover as we read through the recipes both of Levi and Christian we find that they are not consistent. Some refer to hangings and some not; some speak of fans and some not. What exactly, we may reasonably ask ourselves, is going on?

Both the occultist and magician of the 19th century were very much affected by the fashion of the times, and each, as a writer, found himself expected to present mysteries and haunting obscurities rather than clarities. Many occultists found that if they were obscure enough they could attract pupils who wished for explanations and it looks sometimes as if a great many of the writers of occult works of this period made their work obscurantist and sensationalist for entirely commercial reasons. On the other hand it is a principle of all kinds of magic, whether low magic or ceremonial ritual and kabbalistic magic that some matters must be kept secret, or at least disguised, from persons who are not psychologically or intellectually able to make use of them in a proper fashion. It is this which lies behind the same uses of gematria and Notarikon. The clue is, however, always left for those who have studied sufficiently, though it may be buried in a complexity of false indications. Thus it seems to me that the principle behind the use of perfumes and garlands (or fires) in the Levi/Christian/Waite consecration rituals is simply that a perfume which is traditionally appropriate, and garlands which are traditionally appropriate, should be used to reinforce the talisman maker's psychic concentration upon the matter at hand. The same thing applies to the description of the vestments and the jewelry. These accoutrements are simply ways of directing the mind and psyche of the maker into the right track and improving concentration and the ability to visualize what must be visualized in order to energize the talismanic object. Similarly, while it makes perfect sense to make a talisman when the moon is waxing and when the appropriate planet is at full strength in the heavens, it is absurd to become so precise about this as to make it impossible to create a talisman for a given purpose on more than a very few days in the year and at uncomfortable hours of the day or night. Moreover, while again it is sensible to make the talismans of metal, it is not practical to make them always of the absolutely correct metal. The efficient talisman maker can, by means of his own concentrated imagination, "transform" gilt into gold, or leaden color into lead, for the purposes of making the talisman. Whatever one visualizes with intensity is factual in the kind of psychic operation we are discussing.

When we come to the actual verbal magic of the ritual we have no real difficulties, for the words are clear enough and the gestures simple. It is this which is at the heart of the matter, for the ritual is a lucid and definite way of producing the required concentration and of excluding from the mind all intrusive elements. The survey of esoteric talismans, with all its complex names and alphabetical games, does indeed reduce itself to relative simplicity once the principles are observed. It does not really matter if in lettering the name of an angel you make a small spelling mistake, or even if you put down only one of the several available names, as long as you yourself know exactly what your intent is—

and as long as you do not create a symbol so opposite to your intent that even that intent cannot prevent the deep mind from misunderstanding what you are doing.

Chapter 10

The Nature and Use of Talismanic Power

> *Therefore, he that works in magic must be of a constant belief, be credulous, and not at all doubt of the obtaining of the effect; for as a firm and strong belief doth work wonderful things, although it be in false works—so distrust and doubting doth dissipate and break the virtue of the mind of the worker, which is the medium betwixt both extremes; whence it happens that he is frustrated of the desired influence of the superiors, which could not be enjoined and united to our labours without a firm and solid virtue of our mind.*
>
> Francis Barrett
> *The Magus*

There is much disagreement about the nature of talismanic power, and about the importance of total accuracy in naming the forces that one desires to provide that power. Some authorities emphasize the importance of following elaborate rituals exactly to the letter: they believe that the angels, intelligences, and spirits have the same kind of reality as human beings, and must therefore be invoked and bound by exactly the correct name, and even that the name should be written in a language they can comprehend (this usually being taken to be Hebrew, or one of the magical alphabets). There is another view which states that the angels, intelligences and powers of the cosmos are also the angels, intelligences and powers within us. In this view, man is indeed a microcosm, and by calling upon the name Raphael or Ophiel, or Aniel, we are summoning powers up from our own deep mind, and giving them, for the purposes of acting upon external reality, an external form. This form is pictured in letters, formed in sound, and given body by the physical accompaniments of perfume and the use of the four elements air, water, earth and fire. If this is the case, then the intent of the magician is to be much more in control of the situation than others would have us believe. Many commentators maintain that all the occult systems are quite simply externalizations in terms of names, numbers, and signs of entirely inward powers. Whatever we make in talismanic art, or what we perform in magic, alchemy, or any other occult system we are simply looking into ourselves as in a mirror and seeing, gradually, more and more of the nature of man.

Whatever view one takes it seems clear that talisman making can be as complex and mind-boggling and as embedded in ritual and ceremony as one wishes it to be. It is also possible that the more complex the procedure becomes, the less it is likely to succeed for the more doubts and hesitations will be felt by the talisman maker and the less forceful will his concentration be. Nevertheless, there are certainly some people who find that it is only by means of lengthy preparation and long rituals that they can achieve the psychic "high" necessary to magical performance. They cannot, as it were, perform *King Lear* in modern dress on an empty stage.

Whether or not elaborate rituals of consecration are involved, the orthodox practical Kabbalist would maintain that only by invoking the correct powers and calling them into one's service, can a talisman be created. The powers are those spiritual forces which animate and direct us; but they are also forces we ourselves animate and direct. When we make up a name for an intuition, for an idea, for a spiritual hypothesis, we ourselves give the other, the energy, a form in our minds, and by treating that form as if it had power we give it power. We do indeed create the powers we use, though we may prefer to regard ourselves as invoking already existing powers. To some extent, of course, we do. When we invoke the name of a power whose name has been used before by others we are moving along a well trodden path and one which our deep minds find no difficulty in traveling. Moreover if we invoke, for example, the power of Venus, we already have a vision of that power; we have indeed been helped to it by many artists, writers and visionaries. We may still be conjuring up powers that are part of our own deepest selves, but we are doing so with the assistance of our conscious minds that have a vocabulary of terms and a whole series of myths and religious beliefs and legends that enable us to give form to those powers and to name them in a fashion convincing to us both consciously and subconsciously.

If this is the case then it may not be necessary for those who wish to create talismans to go through all the elaborate rituals set down by Eliphas Levi and the Kabbalists. One may indeed reach the conclusion that the Catch 22 which applies to so many esoteric works on the Kabbalah can be answered by another statement: "Only if you know it do you need to use it, and if you truly need to use it you need not know it." The passionate concentration of true need will create or conjure up or form the power that is required, however few or many of the great names are used. Ultimately, it may be that great learning is its own destruction. There is certainly no end to kabbalistic research, for the seeking out of correspondences, the creation of formulae both ritualistic and numerological, and the construction of new rituals that take into account new discoveries on the plane of the material world and in psychology, can take a lifetime and more. On the other hand, what is truly important about the Kabbalah is the way in which it presents a pattern that can be of use in strengthening our understanding of the importance of spiritual and psychic energy in our lives and in the cosmos.

This said we may reflect that we are saying nothing which the Kabbalah does not itself imply, for in the Tree of the Sephiroth it is clear that knowledge can be both power and paralysis, just as imagination can be both vision and delusion. The word delusion comes in appropriately here, for as we discuss these matters we must be aware that, to many people, talismanic power is a delusion. Here the answer is that given by all the leading writers on talismanic thought from Paracelsus to the present day: *Faith is the key*. Belief in power creates power, and is indeed the heart of that power. If you believe in a power, your belief cannot be a delusion. It may or may not be a strong enough power to perform in the way you desire, but it is nevertheless a power and no falsehood.

We are, however, here faced with the problem of who is doing the believing and who the doubting. If all around me think I am an idiot and the talisman worthless, is that doubt going to affect the power? If we believe that we are dealing in energy fields, the answer must be "Very possibly." This is one reason why many talismans are kept secret, are wrapped in silk, are kept away from contact with other objects that have other energy fields. It is one reason for all the mumbo jumbo and obscurantism of magical practices, for if you cannot understand what I am saying you cannot really doubt it except in an extremely vague and ineffectual fashion. Some objects which have powerful energy fields for some people do not appear to have any energy at all to others. The clairvoyant who can, by holding an object belonging to a person, tell you all about that person and even his whereabouts is someone who can both sense energy fields and interpret forms from them. Another person holding the same object will not be aware of feeling anything. The energy may be there, but ineffective. This is a well-known phenomenon in the history of "bad luck" charms and objects; they affect one person powerfully and another not at all, or not to an extent that can be noted.

Within the field of magic itself this problem is endemic, for, with all the various correspondences to choose from, and all the names of power, it is inevitable that one practical magician is liable to doubt the efficacy of another's chosen ritual. This is yet another reason why groups of occultists have always operated in terms of a steady progression of rituals and initiations which are, to some extent, peculiar to their own society. It is also a reason why the "Book of Shadows" (the term for the book in which societies write down their rituals) is never shown to anyone outside the group. Indeed, initiates are forbidden to show their rituals to outsiders. This secrecy has naturally resulted in a lot of confusion. Only recently have we been permitted to read of many rituals; the authors have decided either that the ban was outdated, or that it is nowadays more important to create a general understanding of kabbalistic magic than to protect the work of a particular society. Nevertheless, it is notable that many of the most significant rituals remain secret.

It may be thought that in discussing kabbalistic societies we are getting too far away from the kind of talismans that are generally accepted by and used by people who have no interest in the Kabbalah or in other esoteric doctrines. What about those organic talismans and found talismans discussed earlier, and what about I.D. talismans? Surely these are another matter.

This may or may not be the case. Obviously the found talisman is not necessarily felt to belong to a mystical system, and rabbits' feet and horseshoes do seem to belong to different categories. And yet, if we see these other talismans in the way that we regard the more esoteric ones, not as being powerful because of what they are, but because they have powerful associations and correspondences with many other talismans, and are, as it were, simply focal points for an enormous energy field, we will find ourselves able to believe in them more strongly and therefore able to give them more power. Let us take the case of the pretty red stone we find on the beach and feel to be "lucky." We now know that this red stone corresponds to the enormous energy force of Mars, of the Sephirah Geburah, and carries with it, therefore, the names of the Archangel Khamael, and the symbol of a chariot-borne warrior, as well as many other correspondences.

It does not matter very much whether or not we are able to be intellectually precise about these correspondences. Indeed we may, quite reasonably, decide that the red stone could correspond not with Mars, but with Scorpio, or with Aries, as Scorpio and Aries are both associated with red. We may, observing the round shape of our pebble, associate it also with the Sun, and therefore with Leo and the Sephirah Tephireth. The important thing, indeed, is not that we need to attempt a kind of academic precision, but that we need to be aware of our talisman as being at the center of a great deal of energy and as being the expression and vehicle of it.

It is, of course, true that some talismanic objects have been given their particular energy field and their direction by historical accident, or by their explicit symbolism. It would be flying in the face of sense to attempt to see the armored strength of Mars in the open Hand of Fatima, for example. Some talismans, too, have been imbued with their energy field and their direction by circumstances so that a charming little object may turn out to have the darkest and most destructive energies. Indeed, any object subjected to powerful emotions or intimately associated with the life of a person is likely to acquire an energy field that may or may not accord with its apparent symbolism, as we have already seen.

This being the case, we are faced with the problem of testing a talisman to discover whether or not it does have a powerful energy field, and in what direction this energy field sends its force. In the absence of a clairvoyant who can give the answer by holding the object in his or her hand, we are obliged to check the talisman out by other methods. We must be first of all clear what questions we want answered. First of all, "Is there a strong energy field here?" Secondly, "What form does it take and what character does it have?"

There are a number of ways of testing the talisman, but perhaps the most effective and the least confusing is that of using a pendulum. We have already discussed briefly the use of talismanic pendulums on page 34.

In order to use a pendulum to determine talismanic power or energy, the talisman should be placed beneath the pendulum and the person holding the pendulum should so rest his or her arm that no accidental movement can be made. If the talisman is "live" the pendulum will begin to swing and will soon swing very rapidly indeed. The person holding the pendulum must, however, make his or her mind a total blank if this test is to work correctly, for it is quite easy, without making any movement at all, to direct the pendulum to move, or to stay still, or to change direction. If the pendulum does indicate the presence of energy, then questions requiring yes or no answers can be asked of it. What the pendulum is doing, of course, is picking up from the operator's deep mind information about the talisman that the conscious mind does not possess and cannot acquire by any other method.

We now have in front of us a talisman, and we have discovered that it has an energy field and we have questioned it about its purpose and power. Our deep mind has responded to it and established a relationship with it. It may be a very elaborate talisman, a golden kamea, a god carved in ivory, a ring inscribed with a name of power, or it may be simply a found pebble, a stone with a hole in it, or a piece of bone. It may be an inscription on paper or parchment or cardboard; it may be a pendant, a buckle, a statue, or even a knife. Whatever form it has, it has an energy field, and if the energy field has been increased and directed for a purpose (either by accident or intent) it is a talisman, and it will affect the lives of those who come into contact with it.

All this, of course, applies to found talismans and not to talismans which we make for ourselves. Nevertheless, we may choose to make our talisman of an already existing object, or use an existing object in its composition. If we do this, we must remember that any object which has for a long time been in close physical contact with a human being is affected by the energy field of that human being to such an extent that clairvoyants are able to tell the nature and character of the owner. In making talismans we must take this into account. We may be able to use this transferred energy positively, or we may have to somehow negate it.

We now realize that, as in all magic, it is hard to provide any talisman for oneself but a protective one. It is a widely-held view (although not always universally accepted) that in talismanic as in verbal magic it is forbidden to bless oneself. One may only defend oneself. Some workers of talismanic magic have made talismans intended to bring them personal power, or to serve entirely selfish ends. Such acts, however, appear to cause disturbances in the deep mind and frequently end up having negative and destructive affects.

How can you make a protective talisman for yourself? You can buy or make one of the traditionally protective talismans already discussed. If you do so, however, you must, in order to bolster your belief in its efficiency, treat it with great care, keep it clean and polished, give it its own silk wrapper or box—in other words, treat it with reverence. You must also, every time you touch it or see it, assert its protective power and express both confidence and gratitude. This will considerably build up its power and ensure that it does not decrease. Protective talismans worn around the neck under the clothing should be caressed frequently—this assists in transferring additional energy.

Traditional talismans may not be available to you. You may not be able to find them in stores or you may not have the materials, the skill or the time to make them. In this situation it is best to sit down quietly and work out exactly what has caused you to feel that you need protection. Let us assume that you feel threatened by the ill will and malice of some of the people around you. You do not wish to hurt anyone who does not intend harm to you; you may even wish to bless those that think kindly of you. What, therefore, is the image you need to create? It is, surely, that of a magical mirror, which will reflect back to the transmitter of "bad vibrations" those same bad vibrations, and will also transmit back the good vibrations of your friends. Having got this far it simply becomes a matter of deciding what kind of mirror and where to put it. I suggest a two-sided polished surface which is concave on one side and convex on the other. It should be two-sided so that if it gets turned around it does not lose its power. The concave side concentrates the image received and sends the force back multiplied, and the convex side diffuses the image it receives and makes it harmless. Mirrors, or rather polished metal, of this kind are not hard to discover. The bowls of some dessert spoons are just such a shape, as are some fishing lures. This protective talisman should be worn as a pendant, but kept out of sight beneath the clothing.

The purification and consecration of this kind of talisman is simple enough. The image itself is so closely related to its function that it is only necessary to think of it performing its duty for it to be effective.

The principle followed here is that of creating a talisman from something that has an appearance which is a metaphor of its psychic function. It would make perfect sense to create a generally protective talisman from anything which looked like a shield, or indeed was a model of one. Here, however, because a shield has an ineffective side it would be best to pin it to yourself as a brooch rather than let it hang free. There are many brooches designed to resemble shields, of course, and it must be remembered that the I.D. talismanic badges worn on the pockets of blazers are very often heraldic shields. It is only necessary to think of the talisman working to set it working. But it should, ideally, be concealed. Just as your own deep mind can recognize and respond to the symbolism so can the deep minds of others, and a protective talisman can be circumvented if it becomes known.

Another kind of talisman that you may make is a magical square. To make your own square simply take the numerological equivalents of the letters in the name you wish to use, according to the system of present day Western numerology. Thus the name Venus using modern Western numerology, would read:

$$22 + 5 + 5 + 3 + 3 = 38$$

This is at least the case if we do not reduce the numbers to single digits. If we do this, however, the 22 becomes 4 and the sum reads:

$$4 + 5 + 5 + 3 + 3 = 20$$

If we use either of these two sequences as the top and the borders of a square and then fill in the other numbers so that each horizontal and vertical column adds up to either 20 or 38 we arrive at

4	5	5	3	3		22	5	5	3	3
5	4	3	5	3		5	22	3	5	3
5	3	4	3	5	or	5	3	22	3	5
3	5	3	4	5		3	5	3	22	5
3	3	5	5	4		3	3	5	5	22

In this square the numerical equivalent of the initial letter of Venus is repeated along one diagonal while the other diagonal spells out the name Venus as do all the sides of the square.

If you wish to embody a text in a magical square the same procedure can be followed. Let us suppose the talisman is one to bring love and affection. Your text might be the words Love Is Come. The numerical equivalent of this is:

$$3 \quad 6 \quad 22 \quad 5 \quad 9 \quad 1 \quad 3 \quad 6 \quad 4 \quad 5 = 64$$

and the square can be constructed as before, or you may choose to construct your square without using the numerical equivalents of the letters, but simply in terms of the number 64. Sixty-four is a square of 8, so you might pick on a square with 8 spaces on each side. Thus your top line could be:

4 5 6 7 9 10 11 12

and this line would be used as the borders of the square and the other spaces filled in so that all the horizontal and vertical columns also add up to 64.

If the number 22 is reduced to 4 then we face a different square, and a sum of 44 instead of 64, though, as 44, if further reduced results in 8, a square of 8 spaces on each side, and a key figure of 8 squared—that is, 64 would also be appropriate. In this particular square, at least as I have chosen to organize it, the actual figure 8, which is the key, does not appear. It could, of course, be made to appear quite easily by making the line read

3 4 5 8 9 10 11 12

but I feel myself that the other sequence seems more interesting. The advantage of making this kind of talisman is that in the making of it you are obliged to concentrate upon the problem it presents and therefore you put a good deal of psychic energy into it. Moreover, as many words could provide the same numerical arrangement, if you do not choose to create a square that actually spells out the name or the text in numbers, you can be assured that the purpose of the talisman will remain hidden from all but a perceptive and ingenious few.[1]

Not all protective talismans need to be kept hidden. Those whose protective intention is not obvious may be worn in full view. Thus one may wear a belt buckle, pendant, or ring that has been imbued with protective power quite openly. Many people are particularly attached to rings, and you will often see a man or a woman abstractedly twisting a ring on his or her finger, and, in some cases, this will be a conscious protective gesture.

Making generally protective talismans for other people is not very different from making them for oneself. The only real

---

[1]In present day society, a talisman can remain hidden if placed in a jacket, skirt, or trouser pocket. Some women may wish to carry one in a special compartment of a purse. The important thing to remember is that the talisman must be touched frequently by the owner in order to increase its vibrations.

difference is that a decision must be made as to whether or not you tell the recipient that it has talismanic power. This can be a difficult decision to make, for if the recipient is told it is a talisman and is skeptical about such matters he or she could easily reduce its power considerably, or even negate it. Moreover, here we are facing the tiresome way in which human relationships change; the talisman we give carries with it something of ourselves, and if the individual to whom it is given decides that we are untrustworthy, the talisman may well lose its power or even reverse its intent. This is something of which most people are aware, however, and many people will not wear gifts received from people they no longer like.

In talking of gift talismans we are approaching the subject of the talisman intended to operate not as a protective device but as a magical spell, with a quite specific intent. This is the problem of the "loaded" gift. The simplest example is the talismanic object we give someone with the intent to keep that person's affection and interest. Such talismans are most effective if they have been worn on the body of the giver for a fairly long period, and have thus collected a good deal of that person's energy field. Rings are most often used in this way. Talismans of this kind may be regarded as little more than remembrances. The talisman maker can imbue this gift with the attributes of a receiving station for it can be given the intent to make it transmit messages to the deep mind of the recipient. Thus one might give a ring to someone and then, when they are far away, use it to transmit love, or, regrettably, hate. More specific messages such as "Turn on the TV set" or "Have a drink on me" only work if the recipient is sensitive telepathically, though they certainly do work. This kind of "loaded" gift is, of course, only a step away from a gift intended to have a specific effect—to arouse desire for the giver, or to cause harm. In these instances, whether the intention is benevolent or malicious, it is wise not to permit the talismanic nature of the gift to be recognized by the recipient, as most people are quicker to detect and resent manipulation of this kind than we sometimes think. Here, of course, we are touching on the "black magic" used by many societies, in which an illness-bringing talisman is buried secretly under the threshold of a person's door, or placed under a bed, or in the chimney. That this kind of talisman can be potent has been shown by many incidents recorded by travelers and anthropologists who have spent time in tribal societies.

Talismans of this "loaded" kind do demand from the maker an enormous amount of concentration of the will, and the talisman maker may feel it necessary to create, with great precision, a consecration ritual to reinforce his intent. Talismans of this kind that are created from scratch may backfire on the maker, if their presence and their nature are discovered. This is shown in many folk tales—for example, when the young princess takes off the talismanic ring, or removes the chain from her neck, she not only breaks the spell upon her but also destroys the witch who placed it.

We have not, in earlier chapters, discussed the talismanic gift intended to do other than protect the wearer. The reason for this omission is simple: the majority of talismans intended to command and bind those to whom they are given, or in whose houses they are hidden, are made with such an elaborate accompaniment of verbal magic that the talisman itself is no more than a vehicle for the message it is ordered to carry. It may even be an object which we would never think of as talismanic at all. When such is the case, the object does not lend itself to being listed in the ranks of talismans *per se*. And yet it may have talismanic power.

Many people are aware of the talismanic power and intent of gifts which do not appear to be talismans in any usual sense of the term. The man who gives his girlfriend a nightgown, or the girl who gives her male friend pajamas, is quite likely to do so with talismanic intent. This is generally recognized in that one does not give gifts of clothing of such intimate nature unless one feels that the recipient already accepts one as a close friend at the very least. If you intend to send any type of talismanic gift with particular intent, you should strengthen the power of the gift by using some of the traditional symbolism already discussed in this book. Clearly color symbolism is relevant here.

You can, of course, make talismans in terms of your own personal symbolism, using the basic designs of the hexagram, the pentagram, and the mandala. Anyone can inscribe upon, around and within these forms all the signs and names that are felt to be most appropriate and most potent, using the techniques of Gematria, Notarikon, or Temura. A personal alphabet to spell out the names, and system of symbols can be constructed. This might, perhaps, lead you to create ideograms not dissimilar to those of the Chinese—a symbol for fatherhood might be a formalized picture of a tree with spreading branches. An image of pregnancy could be a circle with another smaller circle inside it and close to one edge. A symbol for the healing power could be a formalized picture of a hand in whose palm was a circle to represent the Sun and its powerful energy. Most people will prefer using traditional symbols, but there is no absolute necessity to do so. It is the significance of the symbol to the talisman maker that is of the greatest importance, and if a newly created symbol enables you to visualize and energize in an effective fashion, then it is a perfectly satisfactory symbol. It is not necessarily the outward form of the language which carries the message but its inward essence, for it is this which is transmitted either to oneself or to others by way of the talisman.

"All truths lie waiting in all things," said Walt Whitman, and in talismanic magic it is possible to feel that all energy is held within the one talisman and given direction and specific powers by either the passionately felt belief and interest of the maker or the finder.